In and Out the Garbage Pail

Frederick S. Perls, M.D., Ph.D.

A
Gestalt Journal
Publication

In and out the garbage pail
Put I my creation,
Be it lively, be it stale,
Sadness or elation.

Joy and sorrow as I had
Will be re-inspected;
Feeling sane and being mad,
Taken or rejected.

Junk and chaos, come to halt!
'Stead of wild confusion,
Form a meaningful gestalt
At my life's conclusion.

This time I am going to write about me. Rather: whenever anybody writes he writes about himself—more or less. Of course, one can write about so-called objective observations or about concepts and theories, but the observer one way or another is part of those observations. Or he selects what he is observing. Or he obeys the demand of a teacher, in which case his involvement might be very diminished, but somehow still there.

There, I did it again. Pontificating. Never saying: "It is my opinion that. . ."

My name is Friedrich Salomon Perls, in American: Frederick S. Perls, usually called Fritz or Fritz Perls, sometimes Doctor Fritz—writing this down I feel somewhat light and officious. Also wondering for whom I am writing this and most of all, how honest I will be. Oh, I know, I am not called upon to write true confessions, but I would like to be honest for my own sake. What do I have to risk?

I am becoming a public figure. From an obscure lower middle class Jewish boy to a mediocre psychoanalyst to the possible creator of a "new" method of treatment and the exponent of a viable philosophy which could do something for mankind.

Does this mean that I am a do-gooder or that I want to serve mankind? The fact that I formulate the question shows my doubts. I believe that I do what I do for myself, for my interest in solving problems, and most of all for my vanity.

I feel best when I can be a prima donna and can show off my skill of getting rapidly in touch with the essence of a person and his plight. However, there must be another side to me. Whenever something *real* happens I am deeply moved, and whenever I get deeply involved in an encounter with a patient, I forget my audience and their possible admiration completely and then I am *all there*.

I can do this. I can "forget" myself completely. In 1917, for instance, we were lying in quarters near a railway station. When this station was bombed and two ammunition trains were hit, I went in without fear or thought of my skin and, in the midst of the exploding ammunition, attended to the casualties.

There, I did it again. Boasting. Showing off. Perhaps I exaggerate or invent it? What are the limits to one's fantasy life? As Nietzsche put it: Memory and Pride were fighting. Memory said, "It was like that," and Pride said: "It couldn't have been!" And Memory gave in.

I feel on the defensive. The captain of my battalion was an anti-Semite. He had withheld the iron cross before, but this time he had to put in a recommendation, and I got my cross.

What am I doing? Starting a self-torture game? Again showing off. Look, how scrupulously honest I am trying to be!

Ernest Jones once called me an exhibitionist. Not maliciously. He was gentle and liked me.

True, I had some exhibitionist tendencies—even sexual ones—but the peeping interests were always far greater. Furthermore, I don't believe that my need to show off is simply explained by calling it a sexual perversion.

I am sure that in spite of all my boasting I don't think much of myself.

My middle name is Salomon. The wise King Salomon pronounced, "Vanity, all is vanity!"

I can't even boast that I am especially vain. I am sure, however, that most of my showing off is overcompensation. Not only to compensate for my unsureness, but to overcompensate, to hypnotize you into the belief that I am something really extra special. And don't you doubt it!

For many years my wife and I played these "Aren't you impressed by me? Can you beat that?" games until I realized that I always got clobbered and that I could not possibly win. At that time I was still interested in the widespread human folly that it is important, even required, to win.

All this boils down finally to the phenomenon of self-esteem, self-love and self-image.

As with every psychological phenomenon, self-esteem is experienced as a polarity. High self-esteem, pride, glory, feeling ten feet tall, opposes the low: feeling down, worthless, abject, small. The hero opposes the monk.

I still have to read most of Freud's writings. What astonishes me is the fact that with all his preoccupation with sex, he has not seen the relationship of self-esteem to the libido theory. Likewise Sullivan, who specialized in the self-esteem system, apparently missed the connection.

The similarity of the function of this system to the erection and detumescence of the genitals seems obvious to me. The erection of the total personality glowing with pride contrasts with the abject posture of the one who feels low. The touchiness of the chaste spinster is proverbial. In shame the blood rushes into the head and depletes the genitals. In German the genitals are called *die Schamteile*—the parts of shame.

In Freudian terms we could call the libidinal behavior of the self-esteem system a displacement. At the same time we might get a first of the few scanty insights into psychosomatic relationships.

Obviously the erection is primarily a physiological function, while self-esteem is a matter of the "mind": that function (that falsely appears as a locus of happening) which I call fantasy or imagining—creating images.

This leads us directly into the realm of existential philosophy. A clarification of the existential issue will, I believe, shed considerable light on the issue of vanity versus authentic existence, possibly even show a way to cure the split between our social and biological being.

As biological individuals we are animals; as social beings we play roles and games. As animals, we kill to survive; as social beings we kill for glory, greed, and revenge. As biological beings we lead a life connected with, and steeped in, nature; as social beings we carry on an "as if" existence (Vaihinger: *Philosophy of "as if"*) in which there is a considerable confusion of reality, fantasy and pretending.

For modern man the issue boils down to the difference between, and often the incompatibility of, *self*-actualization and self-*concept* or self-*image* actualization.

In 1926 I was assistant to Professor Kurt Goldstein at the Institute for Brain-injured Soldiers. Eventually I will talk more about him. At this point I just want to mention that he used the term self-actualization without my understanding it. When I heard the same expression twenty-five years later from Maslow I still could not quite get it, except that it seemed to be a good thing, something like expressing oneself genuinely, yet at the same time something one could do deliberately. And this would amount to a program, to a concept.

It took me still some more years to understand the nature of self-actualization in terms of Gertrude Stein's "A rose is a rose is a rose."

The self-*concept* actualization was there, for instance, with Freud under the name of ego-ideal. However, Freud used the terms super-ego and ego-ideal interchangeably like sleight of hand. They are absolutely different phenomena. The super-ego is the moralistic, controlling function which could be called an ideal only by a 100% submission-desiring ego. Freud just never made it to the point of understanding the self. He got stuck with the ego. English-speaking people will have another difficulty in following Freud's reasoning. In German, ego is identical with I. In English, ego approaches the significance of the self-esteem system. We can translate "I want recognition" into "My ego needs recognition," but not "I want a piece of bread" into "My ego needs a piece of bread." To our ears this sounds absurd.

Self-actualization is a modest term. It has been glorified and distorted by hippies, artists, and, I am sorry to say, by many humanistic psychologists. It has been put forth as a program and achievement. This is the result of reification, the need to make a *thing* out of a *process.* In this case it even means to deify and glorify a locus, for self indicates merely a "where" of happening, *self* to be contrasted (and making sense only through this contrast) with *otherness.*

Self as indicator, "I do it myself" merely showing that no other one is doing it, has to be written with lower case s. Once it is deified to Self with capital S it easily assumes the place of a part—and a very special part at that—of the total organism. Something approaching the old-fashioned soul or the philosophical essence as the "cause" of that organism.

The opposites are potential and actualization. A wheat germ has the potential of becoming a plant and the wheat plant is its actualization.

Now: self-actualization means the wheat germ will actualize itself as a wheat plant and never as a rye plant.

I have to interrupt here. If this writing is ever published, the editor will probably edit out the following stuff or put it in its proper context.

For me, one of two "problems" of mine belongs under the heading "showing off." The other—the problem of smoking and poisoning myself—can wait. As for the first one, the frequent experience of being bored is connected with "showing off." How it is connected I hope to find out in the course of this writing. I often ask for approval, recognition and admiration during conversations. As a matter of fact, often I push myself forward or bring the talk around to subjects not in order to be brilliant and shine, but to boast about the recognition I, or what I consider the same, Gestalt Therapy is getting.

Boredom also often drives me (see the disowning of responsibility for *my* producing *my* boredom!) to be obnoxious to people or to do some "gloom-casting" or to start flirting and sexy games. This will require more discussion in a different context. One boast belongs here. The *Nation* wrote in an article on Esalen: "And all the girls agree; nobody kisses like Fritz Perls."

Lately I have found a more constructive break from boredom: to sit down and write. Without the feeling of boredom I probably would not sit here and produce sentences on paper.

This sounds like a reversal of certain investigations I made in a mental hospital: namely, that boredom is the result of blocking off genuine interests.

Shall I now draw the conclusion that self-glorification is the genuine interest for which I live, that I slave and labor in the service of the image of the Great Fritz Perls? That I do not actualize my *self*, but a self-*concept*?

This suddenly sounds so righteous to me, and "should-istic" too. Self-concept actualization a sin. Am I turning Puritan?

And so back to the "virtue" of Self-actualization and the *reality* of self-actualization.

Let's take the examples of wheat and rye germs to absurdity.

It is obvious that an eagle's potential will be actualized in roaming the sky, diving down on smaller animals for food, and in building nests.

It is obvious that an elephant's potential will be actualized in size, power and clumsiness.

No eagle will want to be an elephant, no elephant to be an eagle. They "accept" themselves; they accept them-"selves." No, they don't even accept themselves, for this would mean possible rejection. They take themselves for granted. No, they don't even take themselves for granted, for this would imply a possibility of otherness. They just are. They are what they are what they are.

How absurd it would be if they, like humans, had fantasies, dissatisfactions and self-deceptions! How absurd it would be if the elephant, tired of walking the earth, wanted to fly, eat rabbits and lay eggs. And the eagle wanted to have the strength and thick skin of the beast.

Leave this to the human—to try to be something he is not—to have ideals that cannot be reached, to be cursed with perfectionism so as to be safe from criticism, and to open the road to unending mental torture.

The gap between one's potential and its actualization on the one side of the ledger, and the distortion of this authenticity on the other, becomes apparent. "Shouldism" rears its ugly head. We "should" eliminate, disown, repress, negate many features and sources of genuineness and add, pretend, play at, develop roles unsupported by our *élan vital,* resulting in phony behavior of different degrees. Instead of the wholeness of a real person, we have the fragmentation, the conflicts, the unfelt despair of the paper people.

Homeostasis, the subtle mechanism of the self-regulating and self-controlling organism, is replaced by an external superimposed control-madness undermining the survival value of the person and the species. Psychosomatic symptoms, despondency, lassitude and compulsive behavior replace the *joie de vivre*.

The deepest split, long ingrained in our culture and thus taken for granted, is the mind/body dichotomy: the superstition that there is a separation, yet interdependency, of two different kinds of substance, the mental and the physical. An unending row of philosophies have been created asserting that either the idea, spirit or mind causes the body (e.g. Hegel) or that materialistically those phenomena or epiphenomena are the result or superstructure of physical matter (e.g. Marx).

Neither is the case. We *are* organisms, we (that is, some mysterious *I*) do not *have* an organism. We *are* one wholesome unit, but we are at liberty to abstract many aspects from this totality. *Ab*stract, not *sub*tract, not split off. We can abstract, according to our interest, the behavior of that organism or its social function or its physiology or its anatomy or this or that, but we have to stay alert and not take any abstraction for a "part" of the total organism. I've written about the relationship of interest and abstraction, of aspects and gestalt emergence, before. We can have a compositum of abstractions, we can approximate the knowing of a person or a thing, but we never can have the total awareness of (to talk in Kantian language) *das Ding an sich*, the thing itself.

Am I becoming too philosophical? After all, we badly need a new orientation, a new perspective. The need for orientation is a function of the organism. We have eyes, ears and so on, to orient ourselves in the world, and we have the proprioceptive nerves to know what's going on within our skin. To philosophize means to re-orient oneself in one's world. Faith is a philosophy which takes one's framework of reference for granted.

To philosophize is an extreme example of our intellectual games. It belongs essentially to the class of the "fitting" games.

There probably are other games, but I see two kinds that

dominate much of our orientation and actions. The comparing and the fitting games. Abstractions are organismic functions, but once we tear abstractions from their context, isolate them, turn them into symbols and data, then they become material for games. Take punning or crossword puzzles as samples of how far we can remove abstractions from the original context.

The greatest book on games I know is Herman Hesse's *Magister Ludi*, the master of the game. It makes much sense to me to see Bach playing with sounds, forming intricate patterns of themes, devotedly involved in ecstatic prayers.

I can't abide by the dictum that play is bad and seriousness is laudable. The master's scherzos are not serious, yet he is sincere all the same. Cubs and pups are playing. But could they learn to hunt and live without such games?

I am confused.
I want to play my fitting game.
Allergic as I am to inconsistencies, untidy as I am
In habits—my room and clothes—I need the order
In my thoughts
Relating bits and pieces to a whole.
Gestalt and chaos are in fight.
What else is understanding?

Let's start with sex.
The many games that man and woman
And parents with their children play,
From tender touch to rape and kill
The many thousand kinds and hues,
Perverted or in normalcy, the tortures and delighting games.
The end emerges clear enough:
Orgasm is the final aim.
No more control,
The rhythm mounts.
Unthinking nature has its way: a happening without the games.
Surrender to a unison,
A deep withdrawing from the world
And closure of a strong gestalt.

Two stages are involved, so much is clear.
One is the making love in many ways;
And screwing is the other stage.
One is a thousand-splendored thing, sublime and sublimated;
It's *means whereby*, as Dewey says.

Sameness with power that explodes
As animal the *end gain* shows.

The end gain is a blissful calm.
The "nothing" of Nirvana stays but for awhile.
Gestalt is closed and satisfaction sweeps
Throughout the pores of skin and soul.

But life goes on. Another need, another game
Emerges from a fertile void.
An appetite, a task, a hurt
Unhealed, well pushed aside by sex,
Demands attention, cries for your ears.
Wake up and act!
For life goes on, unending stream
Of incomplete gestalten!

Life goes on, so does this book.
For some days I wrote nothing.
Showed the previous pages to some friends,
For I was glad that, out of nothing,
Suddenly I wrote in rhythm
Feelingly transcending dry description.
Like a new style coming up.
From mentioning music to staying in rhythm,
Playing with words, yet at the same time
An image expressing itself,
A total gestalt being projected onto paper.

I've got to write about myself.
I am my lab.
The privacy of your experiences is unknown to me
Except for revelations.
There is no bridge from man to man.
I guess, imagine, empathize, whatever this may mean.
For strangers we are, and strangers we stay
Except for some identities where you and I
In sameness blend together.
Or better still, where you touch me
And I touch you,
When strangeness feels familiar.

Most of the time, we're playing games
And satellite around and round,
Avoiding touch-collision.
I am still playing autistically with rhythms of words,

Struggling to go back to the relevant theme
I wanted to discuss.
I also want to learn
To write in verse.
No verse that rhymes, but rhythmwise
That flows in downs
And up and down,
That flows like water
Rippling soft.
Yet prose, to say what wants to come
To mind and heart.
No science dry
Nor poetry.
Gestalt emerging from a ground.
Life living self.
No plastic death.

But words are social, are they not?
So fumbling down from life of self
To words that play computing games.
Yet playing games with sternest rules
Gives me support and growing skill.
No winning games that jeer defeat!
That is too earnest, close to death!
The joy of new-discovered ways,
The learning of new ways to be,
Inventing what was not before
Or words not spoken hitherto.

"Fritz, take a rest.
You've done enough.
You found your Zen, Tao and truth.
To others, too, you made it clear—
Unending growth of honest strife.
What more do you want?
Still not enough?"

No greed for more, but peaceful rest
That sits not still like frozen cubes.
A rest that moves from within out,
From out within, in rhythm style.
A pendulum that is like time,
A heart that beats, contracts and goes.
Contact—withdrawal, world and self
In supplemental harmony.

"Come, preach to others what you want.
You mean yourself and not the world.
For mirrors are, where you assume
You look through window's light and gloom.
You see yourself, you don't see us.
Project yourself, get rid of thee.
Impoverished self, take back your own,
Become the projection, play it deep.
The role of others is yourself.
Come, take it back and grow some more.
Assimilate what you disowned.

"If you have hate for something there,
This is yourself, though hard to bear.
For you are I and I am thou.
You hate in you what you despise.
You hate yourself and think it's me.
Projections are the damndest thing.
They fuck you up and make you blind.
Blow up to mountains little hills
To justify your prejudice.
Come to your senses. See it clear.
Observe what's real, not your thoughts."

But what is real? Does one know?
Now I am stuck, that much is sure.
The *impasse* symptoms all appear:
Confusion, panic and the whine
"One" can't decide, "it" does not flow.
I promise goods, defend myself.
I want to move, but stuck in mud
Can't lift my boots to go ahead.

Too much in love with rhythm-flow
To let the teacher preach ahead
And sorting out phenomena
That are obscure and need perspective as a light
To clarify what is unknown.

What do we know of games?
What is the opposite?
King Lear on stage, he has no reign
As soon he leaves the Shakespeare-props, the paper crown.
Perhaps he is a drunken bum
Without a penny or a home.

But then the king on stage is lonely too
Without a reign or home.
So, what is real? What is play?
Ask Pirandello, ask Genet.
They know the twilight zone
Of play and truth.
It can be this,
It can be that,
It can be both together.

For playing has a twofold aim
To grow and love a happening.
Or: happiness of growth
Denies stagnation
That comes from sameness and implosion.
The clichés, patterns which don't change
They are secure and safe like death.
The *rigor mortis, rigor vitae*
Are so alike in many ways,
As Freud has seen.
Freud also saw the greatest thing:
That thinking is rehearsing, trying out.

But what are we rehearsing for?
A play, an action? What performance?
Without rehearsing we take risks.
We are spontaneous
Impulsive
Ready to act without the heed
Of dangers
Real, or in fantasy.

Without rehearsing we jump in,
Not testing heat or iciness.
To hell with consequences!
Herolike
With blinders for survival.

But most of us are different.
Afraid of risks, we must make sure
That nothing happens that disturbs
The safe routine from nine to four,
Insurance, pay checks, fixed relationships.
We have rehearsed for social roles
With college learning and degrees
Correct behavior for success.
Thus inching up the ladder to the top,
We play the biggest noise on earth
Misusing power for sadistic aims
Compiling money we don't need.

A stomach ulcer prompts the appetite
A smirk replaces laughter.
Connections better than a friendship puts
A strain on our acting, retrieving vainly
Our soul in Sunday's church and New Year's resolutions.
And there are other sides to it:
The good boy is a spiteful brat
The clean one is compulsive.
The weak one snipes a hidden shot
The helpful turns intruding pest.
The dreams of youth turned nightmare-like
To sour one's existence.
What did we do? What ghastly play ensued
From all that gifted promise?

I take for granted that the sperm
That wins the race of a million sperms
Might not be chosen.
The ovum might select its mate.
(Mechanics don't apply to life)
Life is awareness of its needs,
Its self-supporting feelings. Each cell selects,
Assimilates nutrition from the plasma.
It uses stuff from which to make
The bile, the hormones or the thoughts.
It has a mind, it knows its job.
It has a social conscience.
Its own survival is in tune and serves
The total organism.

Not so the selfish cancer cell
Which takes away what other cells
Require for their living, a criminal
Of micro-life.

The cells know much more
Than what we think in arrogant computing.
Awareness-sensing (that we lost)
Is still intact, if we let be.
The ovum thus might not accept
The most ambitious suitor.

A marriage is perfected.
The uni-cell begins to split, proliferate.
Potential man, self actualizing as beginning man,
Receives support—yes, all support—right
In the mother's womb.
The food, the warmth, the oxygen,
The building stones are there
To structure pre-determined plans from genes.
It swims, it listens, kicks around
For *Lebensraum* to mobilize its muscles.

A painful birth, tremendous change
No shelter, warmth or oxygen.
It has to do some breathing now
For life is breath.
(The logos of the psyche-breath is called *Psychologica*)
The first need to support itself appears.
You want to live, so get your breath,
("Blue baby" is this impasse called,
That patterns many later) For death
Will be if you don't risk
A self-supporting breathing.

Cry out in pain, for cry is breath
To overcome your impasse.
And growth goes on. More self-
Support, more self-support, more self-support
Replaces outside helping.
Support from outside is withdrawn.

You learn to walk and are not carried
You play with sounds, then words
Communicate, express yourself.
You raid the icebox if not fed
You choose your friends, if love recedes
You earn your bread, form own ideas
And take your place among your peers.
Now you are grown
Responsive to existence
No drag to other people.
Not a neurotic who demands
Support from outside sources.

I call neurotic any man
Who uses his potential to
Manipulate the others
Instead of growing up himself.
He takes control, gets power-mad
And mobilizes friends and kin
In places where he's impotent
To use his own resources.
He does so 'cause he cannot stand
Such tensions and frustrations
That go along with growing up.
And: taking risks is risky too
Too fearful to consider.

He thinks he's lost without a help.
He sucks you in, he uses you
Unheeding your requirements.
Manipulating others is an art
Which he acquires early.
He plays some roles, selected well
To domineer the others who believe him.

He forms a character which, watertight
Makes you believe he's genuine
Where expert eyes, well used to tricks
Discover merely phoniness.

What games do our patients play?
What roles do they consider?

Most frequent are dependence games:
"I cannot live without you, dear.
You are so great, so wise, so good.
You solve my problems for a fee
Or better still, for liking me."

The "poor me" game is also known
For being quite effective
To melt a heart that seems withdrawn
And cruel and rejective;
Turn on your easy-flowing tears
My lovely conning cutie
Until mascara runs and smears
Your photogenic beauty.

Blackmailing is another one:
"I hate you now, I kill myself.
I'll be redeemed, but you will have
A lousy reputation."

Transference is a lovely game
That can be played forever.
"I see you as my father, doc
And you'll be dear and clever.
What he has done and has not done!
What he should do and should not do!
What I remember or forget—
Why did I screw my mother?
I'm lying on your lovely couch
For years, decades and centuries
(I should live that long!)
Avoiding touch and meeting you
And so we both play undisturbed
With symbols, insights and taboo."

I am really beginning to enjoy myself.
Especially writing this vignette hitting back at psychoanalysis.
After all, Freud,
I gave you seven of the best years of my life.

I am getting restless. I feel excited about the writing in verse. Especially the last one feels like a climax. There are many more roles and games to be described. Ev Shostrom in *Man the Manipulator* and Eric Berne in *Games People Play* wrote extensive studies on that subject.

As a young man in Germany I wrote, of course, some poetry. Since 1934, when I started to speak English, I have only very rarely a connection with poetry. Now it is very exciting to play with rhythm, and find words that fit the rhythm or feel not clumsy and at the same time express some things that are meaningful to me, and hopefully to you too.

Don't push the river, it flows by itself.

I'm tired now. Let's get together sometime soon and talk about the impasse. . .

The Russians call it the *sick point*, so I have been told. They say that there is a nucleus in the center of a neurosis that cannot be treated. However, the energies around that nucleus can be reorganized and put to socially useful work.

American psychiatry has not explicitly recognized and accepted the *sick point*, in spite of the fact that with all the long-standing therapies by perhaps a hundred different schools a full cure of a neurosis has seldom been effected.

Basically the patient improves and improves and improves, but in principle he maintains his status quo. It could be that the neurosis is a social symptom of a sick society. It could be that, for most therapists, doing therapy is a symptom rather than a vocation: that they externalize their difficulties and work on them out there in other people rather than in themselves.

Indeed many of us see the splinter in other people's eyes rather than the log in our own. "If you have flies in your eyes, you can't see the flies in your eyes." (*Catch 22*)

It could be that a neurosis is mistakenly considered to be a medical problem, that neurosis is considered to be an illness rather than seeing that an illness often is a neurosis: that playing sick is one of the many ways the insecure manipulate the world. This has been frequently formulated as "flight into illness," and the gap between malingering and neurotic illness is narrow indeed. As an army psychiatrist I had plenty of opportunity to study this, especially when lack of confidence demanded the environmental support of a pension.

I consider the neurosis to be a symptom of incomplete maturation. This could possibly mean a shift from the medical to the educational point of view, and it would include a reorientation of the behavioral sciences.

Lawrence Kubie's demand for a new discipline, neither a medical nor psychological doctorate, but an integration of essential courses of medicine, psychology, philosophy and education is pointing in the right direction.

If I would become a "Holy Cow" one day and people would listen to me I certainly would advocate such a discipline as much as I would promote Gestalt communities as an efficient means for producing real people.

From my experience with workshops, I am convinced that in such a place under adequate guidance the participants could, within a few months, discover their potential for actualizing themselves as responsible, ever-growing people and get through that impasse that blocks all chances for such an achievement.

An impasse will manifest itself in different ways, but will in every case be grounded in a fantastic (fantasy-based) distortion of observable reality. A neurotic is incapable of seeing the obvious. He has lost his senses. The healthy person trusts his senses rather than his concepts, his prejudices.

In Anderson's "The Emperor's New Clothes," everybody else is hypnotized, but the child has no delusions. To him the emperor is as naked as he is.

With angry hush the adults frown:
"You can't be so audacious.
The emperor's clothes are beautiful.
You, stupid, just can't see it."

The child is stunned, a world breaks down.
"How can I trust my senses?
They love me not if I can't see!

I need their love more than the truth.
It's hard to swallow, but I take
My lesson in adjustment."

It could have happened otherwise
(Who knows the laws of stories?)
If I allow the child to scream
"The king, the king is naked!"
And neither frowning nor reproach
Repress the child's protesting
He could unmask them as some fools
Who tolerate deception.
Oh, shame on you my fallen king
Self-cheating, cheated cheater!!!

I am discovering that the rhythm of up and down is not enough.
There has to be some thematic movement musically relating the
lines. Now and then I feel it already happening.

A poem should be like a song
Free-floating in a valley
Vibrating like a Chinese gong.

The next line does not want to appear. I'm my scribbling! I do
not want to take time out to rehearse and fit words together. I don't
want to get stuck in having form supersede content. I don't want to
create an impasse by admitting ambitions.

No stress nor strain shall interfere
When I engage in writing
And if a critic should appear
With sneering and with biting
I'll turn around and give him hell
And tell him that I'm itching
To show that I, too, very well
Can do some lovely bitching.

Fritz: (defiantly) So what! So I'm contradicting myself and played some rhyming-fitting games.

Awareness is an ultimate
It is a universal.
Thus far we have just two of them
And both in separation:
The "space" that covers all the "where"
And "time" that answers to the "when"
Minkowski—Einstein made them one
As process, always having some
Extension and duration.

By adding the awareness now
We have a third dimension
Defining matter and declare:
"Accept a new extension:"
A process that is "self"-aware.

$$\left(E = mc^{(FRITZ)}\right)$$

Not, like coal, reflecting light
But iridescent amber
That shines its self-supporting shine
That burns and dies in transformation.

Thus matter seen through eyes of mine
Gets godlike connotation.
And you and I, and I and Thou
Are more than deadly matter;
Participating, we exist
In truly Buddha-nature.

The triple God is ultimate
He is creative power
Of all the universal stuff.
The *prima causa* of the world.
He stretches in eternity
And He expands, is infinite;
He is omniscient, thus aware
Of anything that is to know.

Thus, matter, too, is infinite,
The space of all the spaces.
And time is called eternity—
If we don't cut in pieces
A clock-restricted chunk of it
To measure its duration.

When Berkeley-Whitehead had assumed
That matter has awareness
We know for certain that it's true
And even start to prove it.
You can condition any rat
To get oriented in a maze.
It can now show his little brat
A skill that will be useful for a rodent—

A fact that merely will a-maze
The young behavior student.

Then feed the ground-up brain of it
To any of his fellow rats
This gives him matter knowledge.
He need not go through all that chore
Of trial and of error.
Conditioning is such a bore
(Always awards and terror.)

A tree will grow
And stretch its roots
Towards juicy fertilizer.
Undig that tempting food
And bury it some other place.
Then watch its roots a-bending.
Correction of direction!

We cannot possibly explain
By calling this "mechanics."
Tropism that is sensitive
Alive awareness of its needs
That seems the proper calling.

So we inherit many skills
Of ancestors we cannot trace.
And matter-mind as unity
Is truly organismic.

A molecule will likely have
A tiny, tiny quantum
A billionth of a billionth.
Awareness as such is as yet
Impossible to measure.

The mammals have a special seat
In which awareness is condensed:
The brain, where nerves of many kinds
Communicate awareness.
Awareness is experience—
Experience is awareness.

Without awareness, there is naught
Not even knowledge of the naught.
There is no chance encounter
Of anything with anything
And sensing senses have no place
As to acquire content.
The subject and objective
They cannot melt together.

Awareness is the subjective.
The "whatness" is the object.
And all the media in the world
The sight, the sound, and thoughts, and touch
Are based upon a common ground

Which, denominating, I declare:
The medium of all the media
Is nothing but awareness
That differentiates—as eyes and ears
As kinesthesis, and as touch
And smelling-stinking-smelling.

The omnipresentness of God
Is mirroring awareness.
Experience as phenomenon
Appearing always in the *now*
Is law to me.
A present that presents the presentness
A certainty that truly spells reality.

Reality is nothing but
The sum of all awareness
As you experience here and now.
The ultimate of science thus appears
As Husserl's unit of phenomenon
And Ehrenfeld's discovery:
The irreducible phenomenon of all
Awareness, the one he named
And we still call
GESTALT.

Philosophizing is a drag
And don't you dare deny it.
If you could wade through all that stuff
That in the previous section
Pontificating I displayed
Then you deserve to clarify
What is obscure; what does not fit
Where holes appear and incomplete
Conceptualizing needs repair.

For I am biased and, like you
Have incomplete perspective.
Just vaguely hoping that I can
Create the center of a view
That will embrace consistently
The spheres and things, the disciplines
The mind, the body, medicine
And growing up.
Philosophy
That hopefully will encompass
The humans
And the all.

Already as it stands
The theory
Of nothing but awareness
Has proven its effectiveness.
I could not say "all hell" broke loose
When I published that concept
In nineteen hundred forty two.

But more and many groups have formed
With many funny callings
The T-groups and encounter groups
And sensory awareness.
The microlabs and other tabs
For training in
Trala*ri*tata, sensitivity, sensitivity.
(T'is sounding like an engine—
The music seems to override
A serious discussion.)

Those are not phonies, they mean well
Not always copy-cats, but segment-oriented.
Impossible to give them hell
For using parts so unrelated

To growing up and being whole
Thus missing some important steps
To reach the therapeutic goal:
To center one's existence.

Without a center you despair
Of ever being real.
The hollow man of our time
The plastic robot, living corpse
He will invent a thousand ways
Of being self-destructive.

Without a center we are lost,
We wobble without taking stands.
Yes: unalert, no balanced grace
Yes: jello and rigidity
And clichés and deception
Characterizes modern man
In nineteen hundred sixty.

He has no center, he has death,
A catatonic stupor.
He needs excitement, artifacts
No matter in what strata
Of high or low society
He's spending his existence.

The banker needs his alcohol
The hippy, marijuana
To turn them on and to forget
That with a healthy center
There is excitement strong enough
To be alive
(To be alive)
And creative
(And creative)
And real
(And real)
And in touch
(And in touch)
And all there
And fully aware.

The writing of the last two sections was a strain. The river stopped flowing. I even had to go back and "work" on them deliberately; though finally I had some fun out of the two examples of matter-awareness. Sniping at the behaviorists. I am a behaviorist, too, but in a different sense.

I believe more in *re*conditioning than in conditioning, in learning by discovery rather than by drill and repetition.

All my life I hated drill, overdiscipline and learning by memorizing. I always trusted the "aha!" experience, the shock of recognition.

Even now in prose the river does not flow. I am sitting at my writing desk and instead of a spontaneous letting flow of the sentences I am rehearsing, they are milling around; "What to say?" "How to say it?" In other words, I am stuck again—I don't know whom to address, I've lost touch, too many ideas, building blocks, come crowding in, all needed to complete the structure, the approach I am presenting.

I have a number of unfinished manuscripts. Each time I was stuck with an inconsistency, a gap that appeared in my theory, I abandoned that attempt of a book.

But now I believe that it is as complete as I can make it. I believe that it is a viable theory appropriate to our age.

I see in Freud the Edison of Psychiatry, changing the descriptive to the dynamic and causal approach, and also Prometheus and Lucifer, the bearers of light.

In Freud's time, the Gods as manipulators of the world had handed over their magic power to the forces of nature: heat, gravitation, electricity. Freud himself was captivated by that transition: Eros, the power of love, and Thanatos, the power of inverted destruction. The interest in the physical aspect of the world began to supersede the spiritual, just as in philosophy Marx's materialistic dialectic replaced Hegel's idealistic dialectic.

In our time something tremendous has happened, comparable and similar to the unification of the Gods through Moses—the coming about of electronics. The atom, a building stone in chemistry, becomes the harbor of all energy. The concept of causality, of "why?" collapses and makes room for the inquiry into process and structure, the "how?"

Scientific interest shifts from the history to the behavior of matter, or in our case to the "process and structure of human behavior." Not Freud's discoveries, but his philosophy and technique become obsolete and have to be debunked as barking up the wrong tree, the tree of history-oriented thinking. Even if a thousand analysts would bark louder and louder, this would not make the wrong tree the right one.

By understanding the process nature of the organism and its dependence upon the laws of gestalt dynamics, I accomplished the next step after Freud in the history of psychiatry, and this step spells efficiency.

What the third step will be like we cannot tell, but I have some idle speculations about it. Let me share my fantasies about it with you. All theories and hypotheses are fantasies of models about how the world functions. Once they are verified and applicable to physical reality they themselves assume reality character. Thus the "unconscious" and "libido" are as much realities to the Freudian as "reflex-arc" and "stimulus-response" are to the behaviorists. These terms become articles of faith. To doubt their reality amounts to blasphemy. The same applies to my attitude towards the term "gestalt."

Now my fantasy about the third step goes in the direction of headshrinking and brainwashing. That is shocking, isn't it? We are used to the equation: brainwashing equals propaganda indoctrination, so it seems to clash ferociously with my ideas about authenticity and spontaneity. But wait a minute, save your breath. Washing is cleansing—washing the brain of all the mental muck we are carrying with us. To the propagandist it merely means wiping clean a slate to write other convictions on it. To him it means to drive out the devil to make room for Beelzebub. Not so Freud's and my contentions.

Again, Freud took the first step. Realizing the patient to be out of touch with reality, having lost the *im*mediacy of relating unbiased to the world, realizing that something *inter*mediate disturbed the relationship with the world, he called the disturbing agent the "complex." For instance, a man can't sleep with his wife because the unconscious fantasy of his mother interferes.

Freud dreamed of brainwashing by making conscious the Oedipal situation and "analyzing" it, which for him mostly meant making conscious the "forgotten" memories related to the patient's fixation.

Incredible as it sounds, suspicious Freud trusted the fickle memories. From my experience all those "neurosis-producing traumata" turned out to be *ad hoc* inventions of the patients to justify their existential position. What Freud called a "complex," I call a strong pathological gestalt. Wherever somebody is out of touch with the world, there is a kind of no-man's land, a "DMZ," populated by strong forces to keep *self* and *otherness* apart. Both sides, the self as well as the otherness, are in touch with the *inter*mediate only, and not with each other.

Creative encounter has no place. If you wear a mask, you are in touch with the inside of the mask. Anyone trying to touch you with eyes or hands will merely make contact with the mask. Communication, the basis of human relationships, is impossible.

This intermediate zone is heavily populated with prejudices, complexes, catastrophic expectations, computer activity, perfectionism, compulsions, and think, think, jabber, jabber, jabber, think, think, jabber, jabber, think; words, words, words, twenty-four hours a day.

Do you still object to brainwashing?

I feel rather desperate about this manuscript. I've got a view, looking at a tapestry, nearly completely woven, yet unable to bring across the total picture, the total gestalt. Explanations don't help much towards understanding. I can't give it to you; you may take what I offer, but do I know your appetites?

When I could write in verse I knew you would enjoy swimming with the flow: I knew I would communicate something, a mood, a thrust, even a bit of a dance of words.

I am still stuck and determined to get through this impasse. I am too easily inclined to give up and let go. But to force myself to do something against my inclination likewise does not work out. Thus, suspended between the Scylla of phobia, avoidance, flight, and the Charybdis of chore, strain and effort, what is one to do?

I would not be a phenomenologist if I could not see the obvious, namely the experience of being bogged down. I would not be a Gestaltist if I could not enter the experience of being bogged down with confidence that some figure will emerge from the chaotic background.

And lo! the theme emerges. Organismic self-control versus dictatorial control, authentic control versus authoritarian control. The dynamic of gestalt formation versus the superimposition of manufactured goals. Dominance of life versus the whip of moral prejudices, concerted powerful flow of organismic involvement versus the drag of *shouldism*. I am returning to the human split: the animal versus the social, the spontaneous versus the deliberate.

What kind of built-in self-control does the organism have; what kind of self-regulation enables the organism, those many millions of cells, to cooperate harmoniously? Up to the mechanical age the dichotomy of the organism was perfect. Man was split up into a body and a soul. The soul had a separate existence, often immortal, often entering and taking charge of other bodies via rebirth. With the biological realization that what we call life is the specific function of any organism and that we classify any object without that function as dead, as a thing, some theoretical shifts occurred. Thus dichotomy was not eliminated, but shifted to a somewhat different one, very much in vogue with scientists and lay people alike, the dichotomy of mind and body. The function of the body is being explained by a number of partly contradictory theories: from the penny-in-the-slot machine-like mechanical reflex-arc (the stimulus-reflex bit) to a multitude of biochemical reactions, to a number of mysterious elements which manage the regulation, maintenance, and purposiveness of life. The absoluteness of stimulus-response theory has been debunked by Kurt Goldstein. The chemical aspect is one of several possible abstractions, very interesting and important, but so far not capable of accounting for the instinct theory.

Something is wrong with the instinct theory, otherwise we wouldn't have many authors differing on the numbers and importance of various "instincts."

I am slipping again. Instead of writing down my thoughts and experiences, I behave as if I want to write another textbook and sort out, reformulate, clarify an issue. Actually I wrote about the instinct issue in 1942. My present confusion comes from hesitating about whether or not I can claim originality for my "no-instinct" theory, as if this mattered a damn.

I called the book I wrote in 1942 *Ego, Hunger and Aggression,* a really clumsy title. At that time I wanted to learn typewriting. After a few days of exercising I got bored. So I decided, similarly to this present book, to write whatever wanted to be written. In about two months the whole book was finished and without much editing soon published in Durban, South Africa.

I had come to South Africa in 1934. The arrival of Hitler and my flight to Holland in 1933 had interrupted my training as a psychoanalyst. My analyst at that time was Wilhelm Reich and my supervisors were Otto Fenichel and Karen Horney. From Fenichel I got confusion; from Reich, brazenness; from Horney, human involvement without terminology. In Amsterdam, Holland, I had some more supervision from Karl Landanner, another refugee who had been my wife's psychoanalyst in Frankfurt, Germany. He was a man of considerable warmth who did his best to make the Freudian system more understandable. At least he did not do what I had seen Fenichel and others do: perform an intellectual juggling performance with "latent negative counter-transference," "infantile-libidinal sublimation," etc., a performance which usually made me dizzy and which I could never repeat. No wonder that Fenichel often got impatient with me.

One could not imagine a greater contrast in fortune between our life in Amsterdam and a year later in Johannesburg, South Africa.

In April 1933, I had crossed the German-Dutch border with 100 marks (25 dollars) hidden in my cigarette lighter. In Amsterdam I lived together with quite a number of other refugees in a house provided by the Jewish community.

We were packed rather tightly together. The atmosphere, of course, was subdued. Many had left close relatives behind in Germany. Though the deportations were not yet in full swing, we felt the danger strongly. Like most of the refugees who had left Germany that early, we were sensitive to the war and concentration camp preparations.

Although Lore and our first child had found a home with her parents, I was unsure how safe they were as I was on the Nazi blacklist. They came to Holland a few months later. We found a small attic apartment where we lived for another few months in utter misery.

In the meantime, I tried to make the best out of our charity life, with two people I still hold in my memory.

One was an actor, a real ham. Nothing outstanding about him except for a real skill. He could fart a whole melody. I admired his ability and asked him once for a repeat performance. Then he confessed that he had to tank himself up the day before by eating beans or cabbage.

The other was a young married woman, rather erratic and hysterical. I was one of her two lovers for a while. I would not mention her if it were not for the one time in my life when I really became superstitious and believed in something supernatural—in the power of a "mi-no-ga-me."

My minogame was a Japanese bronze about ten inches long, something between a lizard and a dragon. It was given to me in Berlin not long before Hitler came to power. It was given to me by a famous movie director as a token of appreciation and with the assurance that it was a luck-bringing symbol.

I was skeptical. It had not brought him luck.

It certainly did not bring me luck. Soon I had to flee Germany.

The life in Holland was difficult, especially after my family came over and we lived in that icy apartment in below-freezing weather. We had no work permission. The valuable furniture we finally managed to get out arrived in an open boxcar, badly damaged by rain. The money we got for the furniture and for my library did not last long. Lore had an abortion and subsequent depression. In addition to all this, the young woman I mentioned before started to make trouble.

Then I decided to tempt the gods. I was convinced by then that the minogame was the bringer of ill luck. I gave it to the trouble-maker and, coincidence or not, her rich husband threw her out and she had plenty of other troubles in addition.

At the same time, our situation changed completely. It was as if a curse had been lifted.

Ernest Jones, Freud's friend and biographer, did a magnificent job for the persecuted Jewish psychoanalysts. He had a request for a training analyst in Johannesburg, South Africa. I got this position. I did not ask for any guarantees. Not only did I want to get away from the desperate situation in Amsterdam, I also foresaw the future. I told my friends: "The greatest war of all times is coming. You just can't put enough distance between yourself and Europe."

At that time they thought me mad, but later they complimented me on my foresight.

Another obstacle, the £200 guarantee for the immigration, was quickly and miraculously cleared. Soon we got a loan that covered both that and the cost of the voyage.

The last obstacle was the language barrier. Besides Latin, Greek, and French, I had studied some English in school. I loved French and was quite proficient, but I never took to English. Now I had to learn it, and quick. I used a four-pronged attack: During the three-week voyage on the *Balmoral Castle*, I read any easy and exciting story I could get hold of, such as mysteries. I read on, without bothering about details, guessing from the context what was going on. I also studied grammar and vocabulary through the Langenscheidt self-teaching method. I also overcame my embarrassment and involved crew and passengers in conversation. Later on, I went to the movies and sat through the same picture several times. I have never lost my German accent, which embarrassed me for a long time, but I never bothered to take lessons in diction. Later on, in America, I was often confused by the difference in American and English diction. As they announced in Paris shops: "English spoken, American understood."

We were made very welcome. I established a practice, and founded the South Africa Institute for Psychoanalysis. Within a year's time, we built and owned the first Bauhaus-style house in a posh neighborhood, with tennis court and swimming pool, a nurse (we had another child), a housekeeper, and two native servants.

For the next years, I could indulge in a lot of hobbies: tennis and table tennis. I got my pilot's license. My friends enjoyed going flying with me, though Lore never trusted me with it. My greatest joy was to be alone in the plane, to switch off the engine, and go gliding down in that magnificent silence and aloneness.

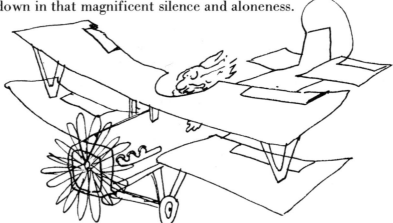

We also had a very large ice-skating rink. How I loved dancing on ice. The wide sweeping movements, the grace and balance cannot be matched by anything. I even won a medal in a competition.

Excursions to the ocean, swimming in the warm waves of the Indian ocean, wild animals galore to be watched, movie-making on a modest scale, directing plays (I had studied under Max Reinhardt) and getting the most out of amateurs, visiting witch doctors, making some inventions, learning to play the viola, building up a valuable stamp collection, having a few very satisfactory and some not so satisfactory love affairs, forming some warm and lasting friendships.

What a difference to our previous life. I had always made enough money to get by and was always engaged in many ways, but never like this. This was an explosion into activity and making and spending of money. Lore used to call me a mixture of a prophet and a bum. There certainly was now a danger of losing both.

I was caught in the rigidity of the psychoanalytic taboos: the exact 50 minute hour, no physical eye and social contact, no personal involvement (counter-transference!). I was caught by all the trimmings of a square, respectable citizen: family, house, servants, making more money than I needed. I was caught in the dichotomy of work and play: Monday to Friday versus the weekend. I just extricated myself through my spite and rebelliousness from becoming a computing corpse like most of the orthodox analysts I knew.

The first break came in 1936, a year of great expectations and great disappointments. I was scheduled to give a paper in Czechoslovakia at the International Psychoanalytic Congress. I wanted to impress with my flying and with a Freud-transcending paper.

I intended to fly, by myself, the 4,000 miles across Africa in my own plane: the first flying analyst. I found a second-hand Gypsy Moth that would make 100 miles an hour. The price was £200 but someone got in and outbid me. So this was out and I had to take a boat.

The paper I presented was on "oral resistances," still written in Freudian terms. The paper found deep disapproval. The verdict, "All resistances are anal" left me dumbfounded. I wanted to contribute to psychoanalytic theory, but I did not realize, at that time, how revolutionary that paper was and how much it would shake and even make invalid some basic foundations of the Master's theory.

Many friends criticize me for my polemic relationship to Freud. "You have so much to say; your position is securely grounded in reality. What is this continuous aggressiveness against Freud? Leave him alone and just do your thing."

I can't do this. Freud, his theories, his influence are much too important for me. My admiration, bewilderment, and vindictiveness are very strong. I am deeply moved by his suffering and courage. I am deeply awed by how much, practically all alone, he achieved with the inadequate mental tools of association-psychology and mechanistically-oriented philosophy. I am deeply grateful for how much I developed through standing up against him.

Sometimes one comes across a statement which, with a shock of recognition, illuminates the darkness of ignorance with a brilliant flash. I had such a "peak" experience as a teenager. Schiller, a much underestimated friend and contemporary of Goethe, wrote:

> Und so lange nicht Philosophy
> Die Welt zusammen haelt,
> Erhaelt Sie das Getriebe
> Durch Hunger und durch Liebe.

(Until the day when philosophy will rule the world, it is being regulated by hunger and by love.)

Freud wrote in the same attitude later: "We are being lived by the forces within ourselves." But then he made an unforgivable blunder in order to save his libido-oriented system. To him the mouth of a new-born had an energy not yet differentiated into a libidinal zone and its functions for food intake. Practically, he dropped the second function and took up a position in opposition to Marx. Marx put sustenance down as man's main drive; Freud brought libido into the foreground. It is not a question of either/or, but of both. For the survival of the individual, sustenance is the important function, for the survival of the species, sex. But is it not artificial to prefer one to the other? Can the species survive without the sustenance of the individual, and would the individual exist without its parents' sex?

All this is so obvious. I am rather embarrassed to mention it at all. And I would not talk about it if it were not for the implications that it harbors for the Marxist as well as the Freudian philosophy.

Wilhelm Reich had tried to combine the two. He made the mistake of attempting to get the two *Weltanschauungen* to relate to each other on a high level of abstraction instead of on the gut level. The result was rejection and name-calling. The Communists rejected him because he was an analyst, and the analysts rejected him because he was a Communist. Instead of a chair with a broader base, he found himself falling between two chairs. He got into trouble through relating two systems before relating his own subsistence and his own sex. He was, so to say, punished for violating some basic laws of general semantics—Korzybski vindicated.

Topdog: Stop talking about Reich. Follow your intentions and stick to your theme, the oral resistances.

Underdog: Shut up. I told you a few times, this is my book, my confessions, my ruminations, my need to clarify what is obscure to me.

Topdog: Look! Your readers will see you as a senile, loquatious rambler.

Underdog: So, we are back again to my *self* versus my *image*. If a reader wants to look over my shoulder, he is welcome, even invited to peep. What's more, I have been more than once prodded to write my memories.

Topdog: Fritz, you are getting defensive.

Underdog: And you are wasting too much of my and the reader's time. So sit still and bide your time and let me keep *you* waiting. Let me be just as I am, and stop your chronic barking.

Topdog: O.K., but I'll be back again when you will least expect me and you *need* guidance from your brain: "Computer, please, direct me."

At present I don't want to think,
I want to be indulging,
A memory in which I see
A pompous figure bulging.
I will return to sex and food
To make your knowledge richer
Right now I feel emerging mood
Of sadness for a teacher.

To understand my appreciation for Reich better we have to go back to my analyst before him, a Hungarian with the name of Harnick. I wish that I could, in some way, describe the state of stupidity and moral cowardice to which his so-called treatment reduced me. Maybe it was not meant to be a treatment. It was, possibly, a didactic analysis to prepare me for the status of an accredited psychoanalyst. But then this was never made clear. All that was stated was: "The therapist had to be free from complexes, anxiety and guilt." Later I heard a rumor that he died in a mental institution. How much psychoanalysis had helped, I could not say.

He believed in passive analysis. This contradictory term means that I went for eighteen months, five times a week, to lie on his couch without being analyzed. In Germany one took a handshake for granted: he would shake my hand neither on arrival nor on departure. Five minutes before the end of the hour he would scratch the floor with his foot to indicate that my allotted time would soon be up.

The most he would speak was about one sentence per week. One of his statements in the beginning was that I appeared to him to be a ladies' man. From then on, the path was given. I filled the void of my couch life with amorous stories to build up the Casanova image he had of me. In order to keep up I had to engage in more and more, mostly phony, adventures. After a year or so I wanted to get away from him. I was too much of a moral coward to come right out with it. After my failure in my analysis with Clara Happel, what would my chances be to ever become an analyst?

At that time Lore pressed for marriage. I knew I was not the marrying type. I was not madly in love with her, but we had many interests in common and often had a good time. When I spoke to Harnick about it he pulled the typical psychoanalytic gimmick: "You are not allowed to make an important decision during your analysis. If you marry, I'll break up your analysis." Being too cowardly to discontinue my couch life on my own responsibility, I put the responsibility on him and exchanged psychoanalysis for marriage.

But I was not ready to give up on psychoanalysis. Always haunted by the fixed idea that it was myself who was too stupid or disturbed, I was determined to lick the problem. In my despair I consulted Karen Horney, one of the few people I really trusted. Her verdict was: "The only analyst that I think could get through to you would be Wilhelm Reich." Thus started the pilgrimage to Wilhelm Reich's couch.

Well, the next year was a completely different story. Reich was vital, alive, rebellious. He was eager to discuss any situation, especially political and sexual ones, yet of course he still analyzed and played the usual genetic tracing games. But with him the importance of facts begins to fade. The interest in attitudes moved more into the foreground. His book *Character Analysis* was a major contribution.

In his seminars I met some lovely people who later on turned out to be good therapists, such as Helmuth Kaiser. Then Hitler struck. Reich, too, had to get out in a hurry. He went to Norway. From then on he seems to have become quite peculiar. Except for having his book translated by one of my South Africa students, Sylvia Beerman, I lost touch with him until I saw him again during the Psychoanalytic Congress in 1936. He was the third disappointment. He sat apart from us and hardly recognized me. He sat there for long intervals, staring and brooding.

Again I lost touch with him until ten years later when I visited him shortly after I came to the States. Then I really got a fright. He was blown up like an immense bullfrog, his facial eczema had become more intense. His voice boomed at me pompously, asking me incredulously: "You have not heard of my discovery, the orgone?" So I inquired. This is what I found:

His first discovery, the muscular armor, was an important step beyond Freud. It brought the abstract notion of resistance down to earth. Resistances now became total organismic functions, and the anal resistance, the tight ass, had to give up its monopoly on resistances.

Another step forward from the couch life was the fact that the therapist now actually got into touch with the patient. The "body" came into its own rights.

Later on, when I worked with some patients who had been treated by Reichians, I usually found some paranoid symptoms, though not severe, and easily coped with. Then I had another look at the armor theory, and I realized that the idea of the armor itself was a paranoid form. It supposes an attack from, and defense against, the environment. The muscular armor actually has the function of a strait-jacket, a safeguard against explosions from *within*. The muscles have assumed an *implosive* function.

My second objection to the armor theory is that it reinforces the Aristotelian-Freudian defecation theory: "Emotions are a nuisance. A catharsis is required to rid the organism of these disturbers of the peace."

Nature is not so wasteful as to create emotions as a nuisance. Without emotions we are dead, bored, uninvolved machines.

The third objection is that these breakthroughs externalize, disown, and project material that could be assimilated and become part of the self. They promote the formation of paranoid features. In other words, the materials that come out in these breakthroughs are still experienced as foreign bodies. All that has been changed is the locale. The chance of growth and becoming more whole-some has been missed.

However, compared with the importance of having made a tremendous step toward a holistic approach, these objections of mine do not amount to too much.

Not so with the invention of the orgone, an invention of Reich's fantasy which by then had gone astray.

I can understand what happened. Having made a verifiable reality out of the notion of resistance, he had to do the same with Freud's main term, libido.

Now resistances do exist, there is no doubt about it, but libido was and is a hypothesized energy, invented by Freud to explain his model of man. Reich hypnotized himself and his patients into the belief of the existence of the orgone as the physical and visible equivalent of libido.

I investigated the function of the orgone-box with a number of owners and invariably found a fallacy: a suggestibility that could be directed in any way I wanted. Reich died in prison rather than give up his fixed ideas. The *enfant terrible* of the Vienna Institute turned out to be a genius, only to eclipse himself as a "mad scientist."

To write about the fourth disappointment, my meeting with Freud, is more difficult. No, this is not true. I anticipated that it would be more difficult, because in my exhibitionistic period I was often vague about it and pretended that I knew more of Freud than was actually the case. The fact is that, except for S. Friedlander and K. Goldstein, my meetings with such famous people as Einstein, Jung, Adler, Jan Smuts, Marlene Dietrich and Freud were casual encounters. They were casual encounters, mostly resulting in nothing but providing some material for boasting and indirectly impressing my audience with my own importance—glamor often overshadowing vision and judgement.

I spent one afternoon with Albert Einstein: unpretentiousness, warmth, some false political predictions. I soon lost my self-consciousness, a rare treat for me at that time. I still love to quote a statement of his: "Two things are infinite, the universe and human stupidity, and I am not yet completely sure about the universe."

My meeting with Sigmund Freud, in contrast, turned out to be 1936 disappointment number four.

I had been in Vienna before. I went there in 1927 upon a suggestion from Clara Happel. I had been with her in analysis in Frankfurt for about a year. One day, to my surprise, she declared that my analysis was finished. I should go to Vienna to do control work.

I was glad, but skeptical. I didn't feel finished and the fact that the verdict coincided with the time when my money ran out did not contribute any conviction.

I had met Lore that year. Apparently, at the University, I appeared to her and some of the other girls as a marriageable bachelor. It was time to escape the tentacles of the threatening marriage octopus. It never dawned on me that Lore would catch up with me wherever I went.

Vienna, city of my dreams—or shall we say, city of my night-mares?

I went to Vienna with no money; I had no resources and did not earn much. When I had money, I liked to spend it, and when I had none, I could get by with next to nothing. Clara Happel, I am grateful to say, had not cured me of my restless gypsy nature. I took a cheap furnished room in the *Eisengasse*, only to abandon it very quickly for two reasons.

One, as the story goes, was a dead cockroach in my bed, a fact that would not have bothered me *per se*. But the dozens of relatives that came to express their sorrow! No, no, no.

And then, the verdict of my landlady who said:

"No lady visitors after 10 o'clock."

"Why just 10 o'clock?"

"Well, before 10 o'clock something might happen. After 10 something is bound to happen!"

There was no argument against this type of reasoning. Freud had a name for it: *Suppen Knödellogik—Matzohball* logic.

I found Vienna rather depressing.

In Berlin I had many friends and much excitement. We fools believed we could build a new world without wars. In Frankfurt I felt a belonging—not completely, more fringelike—to the existential, Gestalt group which had a center there. The psychoanalysis with Happel was more a "must," a fixed idea, a compulsive regularity, with some—but not many—experiences.

In Vienna, psychoanalysis was the center for me. I fell superficially in love with a beautiful young doctor in training. She was like the whole Freudian clique, beset with taboos. It was as if all the Viennese hypocritical Catholics had invaded the "Jewish science" practitioners.

It is difficult for me to write about that year in Vienna. Before this, I wrote the last fifteen pages without effort, between seminar hours. I finally got so excited about writing that "it" seemed to have taken me over. I see that I spoke several times about a center—I don't know, should I spell it center or centre? Both seem to fit. So far, the last week of writing seems to form my center, the excitement shifting from movie- and tape-making to self-expression. Writing in verse has disappeared. Ha! Not true, not completely. Here is an interesting contradiction: My contempt for poetry is vanishing. I experience Esalen, this beautiful place of ours and my seminarians (I have a four-week-long workshop going) poetically. I don't have that feeling for my present biographical spell. Last week I wrote a poem for the girls in the reception office and I don't consider this to be poetic. I have, now and then, in my fantasy, a poem forming on death versus dying. This would be a theme worthy of poetry. Yet the lines I wrote for the girls, who are always inundated by visitors with endless questions, were fun to write. We even used those lines for the "Fritz" film which Larry Booth is making. What's more, I was pleased to hear the replay: Good enunciation and feeling. Not too much of my heavy Berlin accent.

You want to hear that poem?

"Of course!"

Well, if you insist, I will gladly comply.

The Devil's Game.

There is a place like Eden
Where you have miscellaneous
Enjoyments like the maiden,
The baths, the sun and wisdom groups
It's truly Esaleneous.

A devil comes along and prays:
"I also want employment.
I wrote some lovely torture plays
To foster my enjoyment.

"Some silly questions which I ask
Will set you quick a-cringy
If you consider this your task
To answer, not too stingy."

An angel sounds a silver bell:
"Oh God, don't be so furious,
The devil really means so well!
He merely is . . . just curious."

I hope you like it as much as I do.

Well, this showing off did not help. I am still reluctant to go back to Vienna, 1927. What makes me so phobic about Vienna? Anything special that I am ashamed of? I went to Vienna a few times in the last 10 years. I enjoy the opera, the theatre, the cafes, the food.

The fog begins to lift. In spite of their reputation, *die Wiener Mäderln*, the Viennese maidens, did not attract me especially. Never did I have an affair in Vienna. There was very little in between the extremes of bourgeois Puritanism and prostitution there. The free and easy entering into a sexual relationship I knew so well from Berlin and Frankfurt was missing.

I took an assistantship at the mental hospital where Wagner-Jauregg, famous for his malaria treatment for cerebral syphilis, and Paul Schilder were my bosses. Schilder was bright and had quite a good understanding of the structure/function/relationships of the organism. I did not feel comfortable sitting through his lectures. His falsetto voice and disturbed movements made me cringe. Yet there was something lovable and honest about him. Another psychoanalyst who left an impression on me was Paul Federn, especially a sentence of his during a lecture. Imagine a very dignified patriarchal figure saying: *"Man kann gar nicht genug vögeln."* (You just can't fuck enough.) This was in an atmosphere where usually only mind-fucking was esteemed.

When I met him later in New York, we had many discussions about the nature of the ego. He saw the ego as a reality; I have the position that the "I" is merely an identification symbol. What this means I am not willing to discuss right now.

My supervisors were Helene Deutsch and Hirschman, a warm easy-going man. When I asked him once what he thought about the different para-Freudian schools that were developing, his answer was: "They all make money."

Helene Deutsch, on the other hand, seemed to me very beautiful and cold. Once I gave her a present and instead of a "thank you" I got an interpretation in return.

The Master was there, somewhere in the background. To meet him would have been too presumptuous. I had not yet earned such a privilege.

In 1936 I thought I had. Was I not the mainspring for the creation of one of his institutes and did I not come 4,000 miles to attend his congress? (I am itching to write *His* congress.)

I made an appointment, was received by an elderly woman (I believe his sister) and waited. Then a door opened about 2½ feet wide and there he was, before my eyes. It seemed strange that he would not leave the door frame, but at that time I knew nothing about his phobias.

"I came from South Africa to give a paper and to see you."

"Well, and when are you going back?" he said. I don't remember the rest of the (perhaps four-minute long) conversation. I was shocked and disappointed.

One of his sons was delegated to take me to dinner. We had my favorite dish, roast goose.

I had expected a quick "hurt" reaction, but I was merely numbed. Then slowly, slowly, the stock phrases came; "I'll show you—you can't do this to me. This is what I get for my loyalty in my discussions with Kurt Goldstein."

Even in the last few years, with a much more balanced mind, this remains one of the four main unfinished situations of my life. I cannot hold a tune very well, though I am getting better. I never made a parachute jump. I never went skin diving (though I discovered a school in Monterey and may still learn to do it). And last, but not least, to have a man-to-man encounter with Freud and to show him the mistakes he made.

This great need came out as a surprise during a kind of clowning session with a trainee recently. That session was, like hundreds of them, videotaped and, like some, transcribed into a 16mm film.

My break with the Freudians came a few years later, but the ghost was never completely laid.

Rest in peace, Freud, you stubborn saint-devil-genius.

This is the story of my *four* disappointments in the year of our Lord 1936.

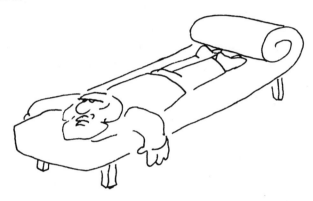

The 1936 trip to Europe was by no means all disappointment, and not everybody turned against me, but only very few were with me. I felt approval, for instance, from Ernest Jones, my sponsor for South Africa. He even seemed enthusiastic about some remarks I contributed to a discussion of anxiety.

After the congress, we spent a few days in the Hungarian mountains. He remarked during a chess game, "How can a person be so patient?" I hugged that compliment to my slightly caved-in bosom.

I don't remember how I got back to Johannesburg. Probably by boat, as in that corner of the world the airlines were not yet well-established. My self-esteem was bruised and I felt free at the same time. Between my poles of worthlessness and arrogance, something like a center of confidence seemed to grow. No, that's not true. That confidence was often there, but unacknowledged. Mostly I took it for granted that I knew what I wanted. I was shaken when I was taken by surprise by some awe-inspiring divine-like device that made me humble and small. It could be the emperor or it could be a Freud;

a great actress did it, or an inspiring thought; a heroic action, a daring crime, or a language I don't understand makes me pray with admiration.

On my trip out, the passengers—all strangers and remaining strangers for three weeks—made me the sports treasurer. The last day of the voyage, they feted me with "Auld Lang Syne." I had done nothing to deserve it. I was moved to the core, ran into my cabin and cried my heart out. A lonely gypsy bemoaning his lack of belonging?

It's beautiful to see how this writing helps. I had tried to make psychoanalysis my spiritual home, my religion. My reluctance, then, to go along with the Goldstein approach was not a loyalty to Freud, but my fear of being once more without spiritual support.

We are witnessing a disintegration of organized religion in the States. The church as a community center, the priest as the spiritual leader and *Seelsorger* (carer for the souls) are losing their significance. A desperate attempt to salvage God is under way. Many denominations, smoothing out differences that previously were fuel for intense hatred, are calling for inter-denominational understanding. "Ministers of the world, unite!" "Unite to deny Nietzsche's verdict that God is dead!" Many ministers begin to rely on psychotherapy more than on prayers.

As a child, I witnessed a similar disintegration of the Jewish religion. My mother's parents obeyed the orthodox customs. Here was a family with strange and often warm and beautiful events. My parents, especially my father, were "assimilated" Jews. That is, he compromised between being ashamed of his background and holding onto some of the customs—going to temple on the high holidays, in case there was a God somewhere around. I could not go along with this hypocrisy, and rather early declared myself an atheist. Neither science nor nature, philosophy nor Marxism could fill the void of a spiritual home. Today I know that I expected psychoanalysis to do this for me.

After 1936, I had tried to re-orient myself. The dammed-up and unexpressed doubts about the Freudian system spread and engulfed me. I became a skeptic, nearly a nihilist—a negator of everything. Buddhism—Zen—a religion without a God? True, I accepted then much of Zen, in a cold, intellectual way.

Then the enlightenment came: No more spiritual, moral, financial support from any source! All religions were man-made crudities, all philosophies were man-made intellectual fitting games. I had to take all responsibility for my existence myself.

I had trapped myself. Through being preoccupied with psycho-analysis in Frankfurt, I remained uninvolved with the existentialists there: Buber, Tillich, Scheler. This much had penetrated: existential philosophy demands taking responsibility for one's existence. But which of the existential schools has the Truth with a capital T?

Skeptically, I searched further and this is where I stand now. In spite of all the anti-conceptual and pro-phenomenological bias, no existential philosphy stands on its own legs. I am not even talking about the typical American existentialist who preaches and bullshits about existence but walks the earth as a dead, conceptualizing computer. No, I am talking about the basic existentialists. Is there anyone who does not need external, mostly conceptual support?

What is Tillich without his Protestantism, Buber without his Chassidism, Marcel without Catholicism? Can you imagine Sartre without support from his Communist ideas, Heidegger without support from language, or Binswanger without psychoanalysis?

Is there then no possibility of an ontic orientation where *Dasein*—the fact and means of our existence—manifests itself, understandable without explanatoriness; a way to see the world not through the bias of any concept, but where we understand the bias of conceptualizing; a perspective where we are not satisfied to take an abstraction for a whole picture—where, for instance, the physical aspect is taken as all there is?

There is indeed! Surprisingly enough, it comes from a direction which never claimed the status of a philosophy. It comes from a science which is neatly tucked away in our colleges; it comes from an approach called—Gestalt psychology.

Gestalt! How can I bring home that gestalt is not just another man-made concept? How can I tell that gestalt is—and not only for psychology—something that is inherent in nature?

If, at the time of the gods or the different forms of energies, someone would have come up with the statement that all energies are invested in the smallest indivisible particle—called an atom—he would have been a laughingstock of the world. Today it is taken for granted that atomic energy is the energy of energies. The atomic bomb sure is a reality.

I can very well understand that you might not follow me in the theory that everything is awareness, but I cannot accept your reluctance about the gestalt idea, and I will patiently describe some aspects of its significance.

But first for station identification: 1926, Frankfurt—Kurt Goldstein, Clara Happel, Lore, and now Professor Gelb, lecturer in Gestalt psychology, a pupil of Wertheimer and Köhler.

I'm playing with the number "6":
1896 My parents move from a Jewish neighborhood into the center of Berlin, into a more fashionable part. I have no memories before that time.

1906 *Bar Mitzvah*, puberty crisis. I am a very bad boy and cause my parents plenty of trouble.

1916 I join the German army.

1926 Frankfurt.

1936 Psychoanalytic Congress.

1946 Immigration to the United States.

1956 Miami, Florida. Involvement with Marty, the most significant woman in my life.

1966 Gestalt Therapy is on the map. I finally find a community, a place of being: Esalen.

I added one more name to the significant people in Frankfurt. Professor Gelb—I have forgotten his Christian name. Of course, I could pick up the telephone and ask Lore, who was involved to the degree of a doctoral dissertation on Farben constancy. No, that's not right—I can't reach her just now. She is in Tampa giving a workshop, probably with the American Academy of Psychotherapists.

Gelb was a rather colorless person, but a good teacher. He is known for his work on brain injuries with Goldstein, especially on the case of Schneider. Their discovery was that a brain injury did not only mean the loss of certain faculties, but that the *total* personality undergoes a change. A regression, a de-differentiation takes place. Most significant, the patient loses the ability to think and understand in abstract terms and language. He acquires the innocence of a small child. For instance, he cannot lie. You ask him to repeat the sentence, "Snow is black," and he would not do it and nothing in the world could make him do it. He would stubbornly stick to the reply, "Snow is white."

My relation to the gestalt psychologists was a peculiar one. I admired a lot of their work, especially the early work of Kurt Lewin. I could not go along when they became logical positivists. I have not read any of their textbooks, only some papers of Lewin, Wertheimer, and Köhler. Most important for me was the idea of the unfinished situation, the incomplete gestalt. The academic Gestaltists of course never accepted me. I certainly was not a pure Gestaltist.

My prominent fantasy was that they were all alchemists looking for gold, for complete verification, and that I was satisfied to use the less impressive but more useful products that fell by the wayside.

A gestalt is an irreducible phenomenon. It is an essence that is there and that disappears if the whole is broken up into its components.

Something very interesting happened just now. I was rehearsing about how to explain this gestalt principle in the example of the water molecule—H_2O and its parts, H and O atoms—when I realized that the formulation as expressed by the Gestaltists cannot possibly be correct. They say that the whole is more than the parts. In other words, something is added to the world simply by a configuration. This would ruin our picture of the energy balance of the universe. *Some*thing would be created out of *no*thing, an idea that would even transcend God's creative power. For it is written that God created the world out of *tohu wawohu*, out of chaos. Shall we then let the Gestaltists attribute to gestalt formation more power than our pious ancestors gave to God?

Before we allow this to happen, let's have another look and, even if this is merely my fantasy, let's try another explanation. I am neither a chemist nor a physicist, so I might be way off. $2H + O = H_2O$ as a formula, is correct; as a reality, it is false. If you try to mix the two gases oxygen and hydrogen, nothing happens. If you add temperature, they explode, give up their status as atoms, and form the molecular gestalt H_2O, or water. In this case, the gestalt is dynamically speaking less than the parts, namely minus the heat which is produced. Likewise, to separate the atoms, to break down the gestalt, you have to add electricity, to give the atoms a separate existence. We can draw several conclusions from that. Without the electronic support, and once they have given up their innate heat energy, these atoms lose their independence and have to create an alliance. This integration, alliance, might not be a symptom of strength, but of weakness.

The Gestaltist might disagree: "Look at this motor engine. The whole is more than the parts. Even if you have surplus parts—extra sparkplugs and pistons, etc.—they are nothing compared to the engine." I disagree. I accept the functioning motor as one gestalt, and I accept the unassembled parts as another gestalt—maybe merchandise, or junk, or potential engine—according to the context, the background in which they appear. Certainly not a strong gestalt, except maybe if the parts would be heaped in the middle of a living room.

There exists a most interesting contribution of the Gestaltists to our understanding: the differentiation of the gestalt into figure and background. This contribution relates to semantics, or the meaning of meaning.

Usually, if we think of meaning, we have two opposite opinions—the objective and the subjective. The objective one says a thing or a word *has* one or several meanings which can be nailed down by definition—otherwise dictionaries could not make a living.

The other, the subjective opinion, is the "Alice in Wonderland" one, saying, "A word means just what I mean it to mean." Neither is tenable. A meaning does not exist. A meaning is a creative process, a performance in the here and now. This act of creation can be habitual and so quick that we cannot trace it, or it can require hours of discussion. In every case, a meaning is created by relating a figure, the foreground, to the background against which the figure appears. The background is often called context, connection, or situation. To tear a statement out of its context easily leads to falsehood. In *Ego, Hunger, and Aggression* I wrote extensively about this issue. No clear communication is possible without clear understanding of this figure/background relationship. It is as if you are expected to listen to a radio when the signal (for instance, words) is drowned out by a loud background noise (static).

Perhaps the most interesting and important property of the gestalt is its dynamic—the need of a strong gestalt to come to a closure. Every day we experience this dynamic many times. The best name for the incomplete gestalt is the unfinished situation.

I want to make very clear a fallacy of Freud's, and to compare this fallacy with the academic and my personal gestalt approach, and to cut through some superficial similarities. In this context, I want to show the therapeutic hopelessness of the Freudian (and every) instinct theory.

Freud observed that some of his patients showed a need to repeat a pattern of experiences over and over again. Some, for instance, sabotaged themselves at the moment of success. He named such an attitude "compulsive repetition." This is certainly a valid observation and an adequate term. Repetitive nightmares and similar gestalten are easily traced in many neuroses. It is doubtful whether we should include in this category the need to go five days a week to the same analyst at the same time to the same place on the same couch, come rain or come sunshine, whether sad or gay, disturbed or calm.

Freud ended up with his theory that life is a conflict between Eros and Thanatos. As each one of us participates in life, he participates, according to this theory, in Thanatos, the death instinct. That means that each one of us suffers from compulsive repetition.

This seems to be a supposition that is rather far stretched.

How does one come from a compulsive repetition to a death instinct? (How does the spinach get on the roof? A cow can't fly!) A simple sleight of hand, Gentlemen! You see, here is this repetition— now this repetition is a habit. A habit deprives you of your freedom to choose. It petrifies your life. Petrifaction is death. *Voila!* Simple, isn't it? Now watch: this death can be life too. If you turn petrifaction outward, it is aggression, which is very much alive. I feel like an s.o.b., but someone has to see the emperor's nakedness.

Where is the fallacy? In the assumption that all habits are petrifactions. Habits are integrated gestalten and, as such, in principle, are economical devices of nature. As Lore once pointed out to me, "good" habits are life-supportive.

If you learn to type, you will have to orient yourself in the beginning about the location of each letter, then move your finger to that key and depress it with a certain amount of force. Your orientation, as well as your manipulation of the keys, will change from strangeness to familiarity, from an unending stream of discovery and re-discovery to certainty—that is, to knowledge. Less and less time and concentration is required, until this skill becomes automatic, becomes a part of self, empties out the foreground and makes room for "thinking," undisturbed by the search for the keys. In other words, "good" habits are part of a growth process, the actualization of a potential skill.

Now it is true that once a habit is formed—once a gestalt is established—it is there and becomes a part of the organism. To change a habit involves pulling that habit out of the background again and investing energy (as we saw with H_2O) to disintegrate or to reorganize the habit.

Freud slipped up by not recognizing the difference between the pathological compulsive repetition and organismic habit formation.

The compulsive repetition cannot empty out the foreground and be assimilated. On the contrary, it remains a constant source of attention and stress just because the gestalt has no closure, just because the situation remains unfinished, just because the wound will not heal.

The compulsive repetition is not death-directed, but life-directed. It is a repeated attempt to cope with a difficult situation. The repetitions are investments towards the completion of a gestalt in order to free one's energies for growth and development. The unfinished situations are holding up the works; they are blocks in the path of maturation.

One of the simplest examples of the unfinished situation is illness. An illness can be finished by cure, by death, or by organismic transformation.

The fact that illness, a distorted form of life, will disappear with cure or death is obvious. And also that an illness, especially if accompanied by pain, will assume the importance of a chronic figure, unwilling to recede into the background, and still less to be assimilated and to disappear permanently from the foreground. This often changes through *organismic transformation*.

If a person is nearly blind, he will invest much effort to retain or improve on what is left of his eyesight. It remains a continually unfinished situation. He is occupied and preoccupied.

Once he is completely blind, the situation mostly changes in a dramatic way. He has got over the fallacy of hope. He is crippled in the eyes of his fellow man, but he himself becomes a different organism, living in a different *Umwelt* (environment), relying on a different way of orientation. He is now an organism without eyes, as we are organisms with two and not ten legs. His chances of becoming content have greatly improved, cf. Helen Keller, who had several handicaps.

If we are not exercising control, if the organism is not controlled by orders, how are we able to function? How is the cooperation of those millions of cells achieved? How are they able to cope with their sustenance and the other exigencies of life? If we reject even the mind/body dichotomy, what miraculous power makes us tick?

Do we have a built-in dictator who is making the decisions, a council of consensus, a government with executive power? Is there an unconscious, or emotions, or a computing brain, which does the job? Is there a God, a soul permeating the body and taking charge of all its requirements and goals with infinite wisdom?

We don't know! We can only make up fantasies, maps, models, working hypotheses, and check out every second as to their correctness and reliability. And if we know, what good will it do?

No theory is valid if there is one exception to it. If we cheat, conceal evidence, we are not scientists but manipulators, hypnotists, mountebanks, or at least propagandists for the aggrandisement of our self-importance.

Out of the fog of ignorance, are there emerging any building stones for a reliable, complete, applicable, and unified theory of man and his functions?

Some, not too many yet. But enough to give us reliable guidance for our specific purposes.

I have made awareness the hub of my approach, recognizing that phenomenology is the primary and indispensible step towards knowing all there is to know.

Without awareness there is nothing.

Without awareness there is emptiness.

The average person is wary of nothingness. He feels there is something uncanny about it. To him it seems absurd to turn to it and use it philosophically.

There are many existents: things, beings, chemicals, the universe, newspapers, and so on, indefinitely. We certainly don't see them all as belonging to the same category.

I don't see many categories of nothing, and I believe it is worthwhile, even required for our purpose, to talk about a few of them. As an example, take the story of the creation.

From all we know, time is infinite, without a beginning or an end. We are already learning to count in billions of years. Man found it impossible to tolerate the idea that there is "nothing" in the beginning. So he invented stories about how the world was created, stories that differ with the different cultures and which conveniently leave out the answer to how the creator was created. These stories fill up a nothing which we could call uncanny emptiness, or void.

Sometimes nothingness takes on a desirable aspect, as when it is experienced in the context of pain, distress, or despair. Shalom, the Hebrew greeting, is peace, absence of conflict. Nirvana is cessation of the trouble of living. Lethe is oblivion, the blotting out of the intolerable.

Sometimes nothingness is the result of destruction, and in psychoanalysis, repression: the an*nihil*ation of unwanted things, people, and memories.

Nothingness in the Western sense can also be contrasted with the Eastern idea of *no-thing-ness*. Things don't exist; every event is a process; the thing is merely a transitory form of an eternal process. Among the pre-Socratic philosophers, it was Heraclitus who held the same ideas: *Panta rei*—all is in flux; we never step into the same river twice.

To call a girl empty-headed is an insult for us. With an oriental, it may be a great compliment; her head is not clogged up, it is open.

My first philosophical encounter with nothingness was the naught, in the form of zero. I found it under the name of *creative indifference* through Sigmund Friedlander.

I recognize three gurus in my life. The first one was S. Friedlander, who called himself a Neo-Kantian. I learned from him the meaning of balance, the zero-center of opposites. The second is Selig, our sculptor and architect at the Esalen Institute. I know that he would be very angry if he knew that I am writing about him. This truly is an intrusion into his privacy. *Ecce homo*! Here is truly a *Mensch,* a human being of complete unpretentiousness, humility, wisdom, and know-how. As a city dweller, I had not much contact with nature. To watch him and his involvement and understanding with humans, animals, and plants, to compare his unobtrusiveness and confidence with my excitability and primadonna-ishness, to feel at last the presence of a man to whom I feel inferior, and finally the feeling of mutual respect and friendship that came about—all of this has helped me to overcome most of my pompousness and phoniness.

My last guru was Mitzie, a beautiful white cat. She taught me the wisdom of the animal.

Twice in my life I have been furious about missing a photographic recording. The first time was when a member of one of my groups had a *déjà vu* experience with trance and *petit mal* (a minor epileptic seizure). We had my video recorder going. I was thrilled at the chance of possibly having taken the only videotape recording of that symptom in existence. In spite of my clear marking, "Don't erase," the tape was erased and re-used.

The other event happened with Mitzie. One morning I woke up and I saw my 2½-foot wide sombrero moving next to my bed. I lifted the hat and there was Mitzie, cradling a bird in her front paws. I felt a shock. Three weeks before, I had seen my living room strewn with feathers, a sure sign that Mitzie had caught and eaten a bird. I took the bird away, her eyes sad. The bird was intact and could fly away after ten minutes recovery. How could I assume that Mitzie was merely affectionate? Who has ever heard of a cat cradling a bird? Without my shock, I could have taken a picture and could have shown off such a rare occurrence.

I know how I got Mitzie, I remember the kindly critical eyes of my early encounters with Selig, but Friedlander is rather submerged in a fog. When my mother mentioned one day the food parcels I had sent him I was surprised. I had totally forgotten. The parcels would belong to the year 1922.

The inflation of the German mark was already increasing in tempo, although it had not yet run away. Food, especially meat, was scarce. My ability to see things in perspective was an asset at that time, just as later on I beat the dangers of the concentration camp and the turmoil of World War II, so I beat inflation.

Jitters about the present dangers of inflation in the States unlock a smile. Inflation! You have no idea what inflation means! If money bears a, let's say, interest of 4%, the law of balance says that that money loses 4% per year of its value, and this is about the degree of your inflation.

Whether the German inflation was manufactured in order to wipe out war debts I could not say, but I suspect it. The fact is that the dollar went from 4 marks quickly to 20, then 100, then 1000 and finally into many 1000's, then ran away to millions of marks and ended up with the price of several billions. The value of the mark came very close to "nothing." I have a historical collection of German stamps from the fragmented kingdoms to the empire through the third Reich until the West Germany/Berlin/East Germany split. The inflation stamps cover several pages of it.

The paper money had to be carried in bags. People rushed to buy something with the money they had earned that day in the evening, because the next morning the value was already halved. Mortgages were not worth the paper they were written on.

Two patients plus my alertness saved this critical situation. One was a banker. I did not know anything about the stock market and its manipulations. One day he suggested I should buy some stock at a price about a hundred times my monthly earning. I told him that he was crazy, but he only smiled: "You can trust me! I will take the risk. You buy the stock now and pay for it in four weeks." So I did, and paid a fifth of its value after a month. I did this once more; then there was no need any more. The respite came from another source, a patient who was a butcher from Bremerhaven.

Soon after the beginning of World War I the food situation in Germany started to deteriorate. Soon the word *Ersatz* (substitute) got an ominous connotation. After the war and especially during the inflation the food situation did not improve at all. A rather funny episode might highlight this.

1919. My friend Franz Jonas and I went for a semester to study in Freiburg. One fine day we went hiking and hopefully to secure some food from some farmers. All we got for our day's effort were two eggs. On our way home we got somewhat drunk and gay. Fooling around he slapped the pocket where I had hidden the eggs, since foraging was forbidden. A mess instead of a precious breakfast! A boiled egg for breakfast in Germany is nearly a status symbol.

Enough of free dissociations! Let's return to my savior, the butcher angel, who fell out of the skies of Bremerhaven right into my consulting room—or shall we say larder? He suffered from headaches and wanted, of course, to be cured, as all neurotics maintain. Bremerhaven was an eight-hour train journey away and he came once a week with a big parcel of meat and sausages. I lived with my parents and sister Else. We never had it so good, as the saying goes. But this was not all. After some weeks he insisted that he felt better, but not cured, and those long train journeys did his head not a bit of good. He had many friends who wanted to consult me and there was no *Nervenarzt* (a kind of neuro-psychiatrist) in Bremerhaven. "I am not interested," I answered, "to be tortured by a joggling railroad coach."

"Well," was his reply, "we could pay you in American dollars." My heart sank. This could not be. Such miracles just did not exist. But it was true.

What the dollar meant during the galloping inflation is hard to grasp. Just one example instead of many. In 1923 I intended to go to the States. I never had the money to have my M.D. diploma printed, which you were only allowed to do after you had paid for the printing of the dissertation. I rarely was interested in medicine per se, and my dissertation was about a silly theme: *Lipodystrophia adiposo-genitalis* or something like that, a rare disease where women looked like kangeroos with big masses of fat above the waist and skinny below. I was not interested in its publication. I went to the *Castellan*, a kind of university purser, and suggested I would give him a dollar if he would get the printing job done. His eyes shone; he did not believe his ears. "A whole dollar?" He took charge and within a week I had my things printed and signed, and had made him deeply grateful without having to lift a finger. Such was the magic of the dollar in 1923.

By that time I was a rich man. I had accumulated 500 dollars for which I could have bought a few apartment buildings in Berlin. Instead of that I used it for a trip to New York.

Bremerhaven had the reputation of being a suburb of New York. It was the German port for one of the two great trans-atlantic lines that had big boats like the *Bremen* and *Europa*. The crews were paid in dollars. For several months I went to Bremerhaven every week for two days, had quite a few patients, using at that time mostly hypnoanalysis, and I had lots of fun besides.

Most of the German M.D.'s were uptight and wore masks of utter respectability. I am sure they frowned on me for those trips. I frowned back. They belonged to the stuck-up, stuck-upper-middle-class-bourgoisie. I and some of my M.D. friends belonged to the Berlin bohemian class that had its hangout in the Cafe of the West and later in the Romanische Cafe.

Many philosophers, writers, painters, political radicals plus a number of hangers-on met there. One of the crowd, of course, was Friedlander, though we met mostly in a painter's studio. Friedlander made his money by writing very humorous stories under the name of Mynona which is anonym spelled backwards. His philosophical work *Creative Indifference* had a tremendous impact on me. As a personality, he was the first man in whose presence I felt humble, bowing in veneration. There was no room for my chronic arrogance.

If I try to rationalize and to sort out what attracted me to Friedlander and his philosophy I experience a whirl of thoughts, feelings and memories. Philosophy was a magic word, something one had to understand to understand oneself and the world, an antidote to my existential confusion and bewilderment. I could always cope with sophistication. The question "How many angels can dance on the point of a needle?" was a cheap cheat, mixing up symbols and things. "What comes first, the chicken or the egg?" not only dismisses the total picture of a continuous process, but specifically leaves out the point of departure, "Which chicken, which egg?" Reich was a typical victim of such messy thinking.

In school we read Sophocles and Plato in the original Greek. I liked the dramatist, but Plato, like so many philosophers, was putting up ideals and demanding ways of behavior which they themselves surely did not follow. I had enough of that hypocrisy through my father who preached one thing and lived another.

As for Socrates, he even surpassed my arrogance by saying: "You all are fools to think that you know something! But I, Socrates, am not a fool. I know that I don't know! This gives me the right to torture you with questions and to show you what a fool you are!" How much glory can you give to the intellect?

The current teaching in psychology was a mixture of physiology and four classes of mind: reason, emotions, willpower, and memory.

I could not even start to mention the one hundred different explanations and purposes that were produced as representing the Truth (with capital T again).

Into this turmoil Friedlander brought a simple way of primary orientation. Whatever is, will differentiate into opposites. If you are caught by one of the opposing forces you are trapped, or at least lopsided. If you stay in the *nothing* of the zero center, you are balanced and in perspective.

Later I realized that this is the Western equivalent of the teaching of Lao-tze.

The orientation of the creative indifference is lucid to me. I have nothing to add to the first chapter of *Ego, Hunger and Aggression*.

Oh boy, am I stuck! That was the only sentence that came. Referring to old stale shit! Pfaw, Fritz, shame on you. One hour ago a session finished heavy, overtherapized. Finally got some resentments out. Black bats leaving the room. Went down to the lodge. They were dancing, turned on, once more over the hump.

Sitting there sad, unresponsive to eye overtures, opening eyes myself, sadness, tiredness, unresponsiveness. It took me sometimes several days to get over a depression. This time I stayed fully with it, resisting the impulse to reach out in false comfort. Today it took only twenty minutes. I am myself again. Pen roving over the paper. It's nearly one o'clock. Last two nights I wrote until three o'clock or so. Up early. Listen to the one o'clock news. We have no FM or TV reception. Only AM with fading and static. At night a classical music program "American Airline" comes through not too badly. We have no newspaper, either. So I listen to one news broadcast if possible. Once a week catching up with the news through *Newsweek*. This week's excitement: we were in *Life* magazine. Feels funny, as if we were becoming respectable. And I have a bad reputation to maintain!

Come off it Fritz, stop that ranting,
Stop that raving.
Be a writer, give the goods.
Poetry is good at times, likewise contemplation
Of your own disturbing moods
And your own elation.
Sit you down and tell us how
Better than a soul, or God
Can creative nothingness
Give us understanding.
Leave that chapter in the bin
With the other garbage.
Pick some samples, illustrate
Give some light to darkness.

Light and darkness—irreconcilable opposites seen from the abstract point of view. How can there be light when there is darkness, the very essence of nothingness? One *ex*cludes the other.

Now look at that tree in sunlight. You see the shadow? Shadow without light, light without shadow?—Impossible! In this case, light and darkness determine each other; they *in*clude each other.

Does an open-air movie theatre show a picture during the daytime? To have foreground figures, we need darkness as background. In order to stay simple, let us stick to a black and white movie. We need the contrast of black and white. We need balanced contrast. Too much contrast and the picture will be hard, too little and it will be flat. Your TV set has adjustments for optimum balance. Again, black and white determine each other. A screen that is completely white *or* black constitutes a *nothing* in regard to its content. The content that is the picture is a differentiation into meaningful black and white dots.

Moving up the ladder, we find Rembrandt, whose juxtaposition of light and darkness is one of the great achievements of art.

Zero is naught, is nothing. A point of indifference, a point from which opposites are born. An indifference that is automatically creative as soon as that differentiation starts. We can randomly select any point at will, and zero-in at that point. If you decide to launch a missile on x/y/z day, you start with a countdown of days, hours, minutes, and seconds, to zero and follow with counting up of seconds, minutes, hours, and days.

A balanced budget is one in which credit and debit add up to zero, whether the budget deals with pennies or millions.

We make a habit of calling the zero point "normal." We then talk about normal temperature, normal bloodcount, etc., *ad infinitum*. Any plus or minus is called abnormal, a sign of malfunctioning—of illness, if the plus or minus is considerable.

In the case of the biological organism, the zero point of normalcy has to be maintained or the organism will stop functioning; the organism will die.

Each cell, each organ, each total organism has a considerable number of normal functions to maintain.

Each cell, each organ, each total organism is busy disposing of any excess (+) and filling up any deficiency (–) in order to maintain the zero point, the point of optimal functioning.

Each cell, each organ, each total organism is in touch with its environment, disposing and replenishing.

Each cell, each organ has an intra-organismic environment (body fluids, nerves, etc.) in which it is embedded. The total organism has the world as environment in which it must maintain the subtle organismic balance.

Any disturbance of the organismic balance constitutes an incomplete gestalt, an unfinished situation forcing the organism to become creative, to find means and ways to restore that balance.

Any deficiency—of calcium, amino acids, oxygen, affection, importance, etc.—produces a need to get those from somewhere. We don't *have* an "instinct" for calcium, amino acids, oxygen, affection, importance, etc., we *create* those thousands of possible "instincts" *ad hoc* whenever a specific balance is disturbed.

Any surplus creates a temporary instinct to get rid of it—carbon dioxide, lactic acid, semen, feces, irritations, resentments, fatigue, etc.—in order to restore the organismic balance.

Each breath replenishes oxygen and disposes of carbon dioxide. Breathing often—lopsidedly—is equated with *in*haling. "Take a breath."

I don't want to wash my hands in a basin half-filled with dirty water. I don't pour fresh water on top of the dirty water. I drain the dirty water first.

To drain the "dirty" air, first *ex*hale! If *in*haling becomes a fetish, you might develop asthma, a desperate attempt of nature to squeeze out used-up air.

I speedily "cured" every psychogenic asthma I came across. In most cases, there was an embarassment behind the asthma, a fear of making those wild exhaling noises that go along with orgasm. Fear of betraying one's masturbation, expectation of discovery of having a lover in bed are preferred occasions to work through. I let them play "fucking." They finished the breathing impasse with some dizziness, and then tremendous relief.

I have a number of so-called miraculous cures in my garbage bin. Here is a lulu I can pull out. These types of cures are as little miracles as the fact that you can see a tree which the blind cannot see. It is merely that my intermediate zone is less crowded than the average and that I am capable of seeing the obvious. I need to mention the following case as an example of imbalance.

A violinist was sent to me for a cramp which he developed in his left hand after playing his instrument only fifteen minutes. He had the ambition to be a soloist; he did not have his cramp while he was playing in the orchestra. All neurological investigation proved to be negative. Obviously this was a psychosomatic case and psychoanalysis was indicated.

I have seen many cases of psychoanalysis of long duration. Five to ten years are quite frequent. But he was tops. He had had twenty-seven years of it with six different therapists. Needless to say, all aspects of the Oedipus complex, masturbation, exhibitionism, etc., were gone over again and again.

When he came to me and made a dive for the couch, I stopped him and asked him to bring his violin along.

"What for?"

"I want to see how you manage to produce this cramp."

He brought his violin and played beautifully, standing up. I saw that he got his support from his right leg and that he had his left leg crossed over. After about ten minutes he began to wobble slightly. This wobble increased imperceptibly, and within a few more minutes his fingering slowed down and many notes were inaccurately played. He interrupted: "You see? It's getting difficult. If I force myself to go on, I get my cramp and I can't play at all."

And you don't get the cramp in the orchestra?

"Never."

Do you sit?

"Of course, but as soloist I have to stand up."

O.K. Now let me massage your hands. Now stand with your feet apart, slightly bent in at your knees. Now start again.

After twenty minutes of perfect playing, tears came to his eyes. He muttered: "I won't believe it, I won't believe it."

By then his hour was over, but I let my next patient wait. This was too important! I wanted to make sure and let him play a few more minutes.

What had happened? We have several polarities which, if not properly balanced, will produce a split and conflict. Most frequent is the right/left dichotomy. Less frequent the front/rear or the upper/under carriage split, first observed by Lore. The part above the waist has essentially contact functions, the lower part supportive functions. Now, my patient had enough support when he was sitting, but standing mostly on his right leg was not enough support for the subtle finger movements of his left hand. As soon as his right leg got tired of carrying the whole load, he began to wobble and he had to regain his balance nearly every second. This imbalance was a strain influencing the upper carriage and especially the left hand. We still had to work some more weeks, not only to wean him from his couch life, but also to soften his "grim determination"—clenched jaws, etc.

I don't know if he ever made it. He played well enough, but I never saw his name announced as one of the star soloists.

At that time, I was already well-established in New York and began to get a name as somebody who was willing and eager to get refractory cases.

Actually, for a while it was touch-and-go if I would stay in the States.

I am at a minor impasse. I feel like writing about my coming to the States, and at the same time, I don't feel too good about it. This shuffling from one context to another begins to feel like a gimmick, like a technique. It is not even counterpoint style, mutually supporting. But then, who else but me is going to set the rules on what to throw into the garbage and what to pick out? What's more, I am not even writing of what is troubling me at the moment.

It is a quarter-past-three in the morning, and I can't sleep. This is a very rare occurrence. Usually I am able to get in touch with and localize any over-excitement. This dissolves and dissipates, the "I" awareness fades, the body awareness diminishes, and then "nothing" until the morning.

Larry Booth has made a film in color, called "Fritz." This film is a poem, a rather exciting portrait of me, though there was some remark that my warmth and love is not coming through as in the films dealing with therapy sessions. This would not bother me. What is upsetting is that I am suspicious and irritable about some paranoid attitude of mine. This has become very rare. I feel I am being taken advantage of. Actually and factually, I am justified as far as the agreement and the financial situation is concerned. But I cannot allow myself to be generous and to experience myself as a sucker. I can afford it. I make good money. So what the hell!

I lived through the terrors of Flanders, I lived through plenty of mudslinging, I lived through that time in Holland, and through many other troubles—still I cannot be rational about it. It is still the arrogant self-concept, "You can't do this to me!"

I had a number of paranoid spells, even in situations where I was in the wrong. These spells were very marked and exaggerated after my first few LSD trips. At those times, I lost my perspective and experienced plenty of revenge fantasies. I know this would be the time to talk about psychedelic drugs and my relation to them, but I begin to feel heavy and tired. I have to postpone it. Will this writing bring me sleep?

At the lunch table today, we spoke about learning. I suggested that learning is discovery. This relates to facts. The learning of skills is the *discovery* that something is possible. To teach is to *show* that something is possible. Discover: to uncover, take a cover away, make the thing or skill appear, to add something "new."

A cell or an organism having lost its center—the zero point, normality, the point of creative indifference—discovers this imbalance and discovers the means of regaining it. This can be a simple or a very complicated process, and it presupposes that at least all organic life has awareness. A water deficiency, for instance, creates a temporary water-instinct called thirst, then discovers a source of water, say a bottle of beer, then discovers a means to open the bottle and then discovers that drinking annihilates the thirst. Expressed as a formula, it says: The state of the organism is $-x$ water. By taking in $+x$ water, we arrive at zero, the disappearance of an imbalance.

With such a formula, we are making a little progress, as compared with making a soul or God or "life" the agent of the organism's functioning. We have already some movement; we have one well-defined relationship of the organism to its environment, and we have introduced a basic organismic function—the necessity to discover.

I feel now the need to defend myself against being called a Behaviorist. In a way, this is true. I am interested in investigating how matter, and specifically how the human being, behaves. The difference between my attitude and the large class of psychologists who call themselves Behaviorists is decisive. It is the difference between a populated place and a ghost town.

Awareness is an experience of utmost privacy. I cannot be *aware* of *your* awareness, I can only indirectly participate. The Behaviorist observes humans and rats "as if" they have no awareness, "as if" they are things. As a result, the Behaviorist becomes an engineer and conditioner of behavior—that is, a controller and a manipulator.

But even he will admit the basic function of discovery. Without being aware of shocks and appetites, no animal would discover: "What is the experimenter's wish for me to behave?"

It is important for me to use terms which cover the whole range of abstractions and fit into everybody's language. It is a pity we don't have some common language term for gestalt—pattern, melody, configuration are already too specific. I believe as we go on the idea of gestalt will come across. I hope this writing will help to finally come up with a good formulation. The understanding of gestalt is simple in the case of a melody. If you transpose a musical theme from one key to another, the theme remains the same although in fact you have changed every note. If you know a melody well and somebody sings the first three notes, you automatically complete the melody.

Thus we are back to one of the basic laws of gestalt formation—the tension arising out of the need for closure is called frustration, the closure is called satisfaction. *Satis*—enough; *facere*—to make: Make it so that you have enough. In other words, fulfillment, fill yourself until you are full. With satisfaction, the imbalance is annihilated, it disappears. The incident is closed.

Just as balance and discovery are met on all levels of existence, so are frustration, satisfaction, and closure.

I am thinking of the situation of prolonged war with its frustrations and the possible closure—peace.

I mean specifically the frustrations of the fighting man, of course, and I am comparing my own situation during World Wars I and II—terror versus a comfortable air-raid shelter.

When the Hitler war broke out, I was well-established in Johannesburg; that is *we* were, because Lore also had a practice. I had not yet broken with the Freudians officially. That came later. As a matter of fact, I can pin down the exact minute when I felt full freedom from those ideological shackles and started to oppose Freud's system. For years I was inclined to overdo this opposition; I lacked the appreciation for Freud and his discoveries.

The break came when I met Maria Bonaparte, Princess of Greece, in Capetown. She was a friend and disciple of Freud's. I had completed and mimeographed the manuscript of *Ego, Hunger and Aggression* and gave it to her to read. When she returned that manuscript, she gave me the shock treatment I needed. She said, "If you don't *believe* in the libido theory any more, you better hand in your resignation." I did not quite trust my ears. A scientific approach based on an article of faith?

She was right, of course. Libido was in some vague way connected with the sexual hormones, but Freud, suffering, like me, from systematitis, had to find a common denominator for his model of man. He called that common denominator the libido. At a closer look, this common denominator was like the joker in a card game. It could stand for a lot of things, be it sex-impulse, affection, sensitivity, love, gestalt formation, *élan vital*. Poor Wilhelm Reich, trying to find an equivalent of this semantic mixture in physical reality.

In any case, I did not hand in my resignation. I was not thrown out; my relationship with the Psychoanalytic Institute, etc., simply petered out. I might have taken a stand if it had not been for the war.

Hitler's Afrika Corps was roaming freely in North Africa. A South African division got caught in Tobruck. I did not know what to do. My M.D. was not valid. I was willing to join up as a medic, but was sent home with the request to take an examination in hygiene. This would grant me a commission. I studied this subject with two friends for several months, but when it came to the examination, they passed and I failed.

Soon after that, a law was passed recognizing foreign degrees for the duration. So I was accepted as a medical officer and went through a training course. We were called the chain gang. We really were a sight. It felt funny to be a soldier again and to be put through the paces. Then we were attached to the hospitals.

Life there was very much routine. I was surprised how much tea we drank. My orderly woke me up with a "nice cup o' tea." Then tea for breakfast, ten o'clock tea, four o'clock tea, dinner tea, and late snack tea.

Our C.O. was a reserve officer and out to prove his efficiency. Everything had to be written in triplicate and registered. After a year, we got rid of him. A regular army colonel took his place. He called us in and said, "Gentlemen, you are officers and doctors. I trust that you are responsible people and know what you are doing. I suggest you use the phone rather than the pen." We felt relieved that he did not suffer from a red tapeworm. The patient turnover doubled in no time.

The head nurse on my ward was a volunteer from Vancouver, a beautiful, tall blonde. She was warm and yet asexual. Quiet, and yet one of the most efficient and reliable persons I ever met in my life. I respected her so much that I never made a pass at her. The fox and his sour grapes? Perhaps.

The patients were, of course, divided according to races. The separation of black and white after the Apartheid in 1946 increased, but don't believe for a moment that under the more liberal regime of Jan Smuts there was anything smelling of equality. The whites were called Europeans and the blacks, natives. No native was allowed to sleep in the same house with a European, or to use the same toilet. They had separate busses and separate townships.

I distinguished basically two forms of mental breakdown among the natives. One belonged to the urbanized native, who usually spoke English or *Afrikaans*, a bastardized form of Dutch. He usually had a severe anxiety neurosis. The raw native, however, who was recruited from the *Kraal* or the mining compounds, had a schizophrenic type of neurosis. I could not deal with him, even through an interpreter. I sent him to his witch doctor; often he came back cured.

The European neuroses could usually be pigeonholed, although this is an oversimplification. Usually the British had character neuroses, the Jews hysteria, and the Boers compulsive features.

Slowly it dawned on my colleagues how much psychosomatic illness existed. The boss of the internal medical department said in the beginning, "Behind every neurosis there is a stomach ulcer." And in the end, "Perls, (the buddy-buddy American custom of first-name calling was frowned upon, except for close friends) you were right: Behind every stomach ulcer there is a neurosis." I was pleased; I even forgave him for a booboo he made with me.

I had an inflammation in my right toe. It was a painful swelling. He diagnosed it as gout, and I was furious. Me and gout, this does not fit! In spite of his medication, the pain became excruciating. I insisted on an x-ray. They found a splinter, apparently left behind from a previous fracture. A small operation and I was fine after a few days.

I had plenty of small injuries from motorcycle riding and other sports, and only one more serious one: a concussion after a very hard fall in the skating rink. Luckily there was no fracture or permanent brain damage.

My first recognition came after one of my so-called miracle cures. A soldier suffered from big welts all over his body. As a last resort, he was sent to me.

A psychiatric diagnosis could never be made simply on the basis of absent neurological or similar findings. There has to be some clear psychological indication. This soldier had a deep despair in his eyes and was somewhat dazed. In the army, of course, we had no time to fool with psychoanalysis or any other extensive form of psychotherapy. I put him under pentothal and learned that he had been in a concentration camp. I spoke German to him and led him back to his moments of despair and removed the crying block. He really cried his heart out, or shall we say he cried his skin out. He woke up in a state of confusion, and then he really woke up and had the typical *satori* experience of being completely and freely in the world. At last he had left the concentration camp behind and was with us. The welts disappeared.

Spectacular cures like this were, of course, rare. Usually there was much drudgery involved if I wanted to make use of psychotherapy at all.

Bang! An interruption. Come in, G. Have a marzipan potato. Grete, my sister, shows me her love by sending me the most exquisite candies. I am stingy about sharing them, but I do.

I told G. the wonderful thing that is beginning to happen. I begin to appreciate myself—my subtleties, my timing, my clarity of vision. What a difference from showing off and boasting. What a difference from my greed for appreciation and its flat and short-lived nourishment.

This morning at the breakfast table—no, already soon after

waking—the whirl started up again. I am groping for something in the fog. In fantasy I am writing furiously. Again, many themes come crowding in, but many themes make a symphony only if structured and integrated.

I see that this writing is developing into a book and probably into a big volume. I never realized how much there is in my garbage bin, and how much has to be disposed of. I know that much of my experience will be valuable to many readers. Already I have had very reassuring feedback from friends to whom I have lent parts of the manuscript.

One remark that I get makes me embarrassed and angry: "When will the book come out?"

"Will you please leave me alone and let me do my thing! I am glad that I am excited and eager to write. I am glad to do something that integrates your needs and mine. So, don't push the river; it flows by itself!"

And if the events and ideas come crowding in, no fantasy, no anticipation, no rehearsing will dictate the flow. The figure/background formation dictates that only one event can occupy the foreground, dominating the situation. Otherwise there is conflict and confusion.

And the figure/background formation which is the strongest will temporarily take over the control of the total organism. Such is the basic law of organismic self-regulation—no specific need, no instinct, purpose, or goal, no deliberate intention will have any influence if it is not backed up by the energizing gestalt.

If more than one gestalt tends to emerge, the unified control and action is in danger. In our example of thirst, it is not the thirst that goes after the water, but the total organism. *I* go after it. The thirst directs *me*.

If more than one gestalt emerges, a split, a dichotomy, an inner conflict might develop, weakening the potential that has to be invested to complete the unfinished situation.

If more than one gestalt emerges, the human being begins to "decide," often to the point of deciding to play the self-torture game of indecisiveness.

If more than one gestalt wants to emerge and nature is left alone, then there will be no decisions, but preferences. Such a process means order instead of conflict.

There is no hierarchy of "instincts;" there is a hierarchy of the emergence of the most urgent gestalt.

After closure this gestalt will recede into the background, to empty the foreground for another emergent or emergency. After one gestalt receives satisfaction, the organism can deal with the next urgent frustration. Always first things first. When a caller, urgent letters or bills, or a seminar session needs my attention, this writing will take a place in the background. It will not disappear, be forgotten or repressed. It will remain in the aliveness of the figure/background exchange.

When my preoccupation with this book remains close to the foreground, I will pay little attention to the chatter at my table or to the beauty of the landscape.

Every interference with the elasticity of the foreground/background interchange brings about neurotic or psychotic phenomena.

Foreground and background have to be easily interchangeable, according to the requirements of my being. If not, we get an accumulation of unfinished situations, fixed ideas, rigid character structure.

Foreground and background must be easily interchangeable. Otherwise we get a disturbance in the attention system—confusion, loss of being in touch, inability to concentrate and to get involved.

Once I read a paper to our hospital staff. I wanted to make it so simple that even the M.D.'s could understand the principle of gestalt formation. I chose a frequent symptom, insomnia, and described the meaning of insomnia as an attempt of the organism to cope with problems that were more important than sleep. A threatening interview of the next day, an unfulfilled revenge, an unexpected resentment, a strong sexual urge are only a few of such unfinished situations that interfere with that withdrawal from the world which we call sleep.

In order to cope with the unfinished situation, the organism has to produce an increased amount of excitement. Over-excitement and sleep are incompatible. Thus, if you can't sleep and you don't apply the excitement towards the incomplete gestalt, then you have to look for another outlet and get angry with the insomnia or the hard pillow or the barking dog. The angrier you get, the less you can sleep. Closing your eyes does not help. Closing of the eyes does not bring sleep; sleep brings on the closing of the eyes.

You might also take refuge in the panacea of modern psychiatry, tranquilizers, the damper of the excitement of our life force, and push your unsolved problems under the rug.

Long live the American way of a life of mediocre excitement, with its complement, violence. Or shall we prescribe a good dose of tranquilizers for each citizen for breakfast?

I am living on the grounds of the Esalen Institute. As usual, I went to bed late and woke up early looking out of the window. The cliffs of Big Sur, restless waves, kelp floating in large brown mats. Last year the slopes from my house were nearly naked. Now all kinds of bushes cover them. Flowers intersperse them, flowing with colors waiting to be painted by Corot or Renoir.

The beach has no sand. It has boulders and rocks waiting for the waves to play with them. And there they come, one after another. Gently creeping, then jumping and dancing, embracing and melting, dying in whiteness.

One of the rocks touching the beach has historical significance. Elizabeth Taylor sat there for a movie. I never went down and worshipped that rock. I have been told—I can't vouch for it—that for the scene the rock was covered with foam rubber and painted over to make it more moviegenic or comfortable or protective against the coldness of the rock. After all, a movie star's ass is probably highly-insured property.

The sea otters playing around there don't seem to appreciate the holiness of that rock. My house is sitting right on the cliff, just three hundred feet above the famous hot sulphur springs which gave us our address. There are about twenty to thirty springs. The temperature is 130°. The sulphur smell is not obnoxious, the water is super soft. The bath houses open onto the sea and a diamond-studded sky at night. Fog is frequent and the rain in winter, heavy. The air temperature is never under freezing and really hot days are rare.

This travelogue does not tell us anything about the role the baths have assumed. Both sides have tubs and plunges. At times, up to sixteen people crowd into one plunge. In the tubs you wash and shampoo. To do this in the plunge is very much frowned upon. At times the sexes are separated, at other times we have joint bathing sessions, usually after the evening seminars. Sometimes encounter groups meet there in the afternoon, and the families of the staff before supper.

I recommend those joint baths to my non-professional groups, but make it a demand for the professionals—psychiatrists, psychologists, ministers, etc. Many of them come uptight, with little self-support apart from their professional role, afraid to come down to us mortals, often unwilling to subscribe to Whittaker's beautiful discovery of the "patient's sector in the therapist." (Too many therapists are still unwilling to admit to, or even to be elevated to, the status of a patient.) They always—I don't think I have seen more than one or two exceptions—are disappointed about the non-

existence of squeamishness and coaxing, and are amazed about the absence of the expected thrill of nudity. You can see anything from quiet relaxed floating to fierce embracing, from community singing to rehashing of seminar sessions. Sometimes they get bored and self-conscious and sink to the low level of joke-telling. They touch each other, mostly in the form of massage. Open sex and violence are rare.

Once there was a real bitch of a girl who played two men against each other. One, apparently in need to show off, spoke wildly and threatened to kill and to run amok. When he came to our plunge I stood up and in spite of my age punched him right in the nose. To my astonishment he collapsed without putting up any resistance and started to cry.

I am rarely afraid. A good psychiatrist has to risk his life and reputation if he wants to achieve something real. He has to take a stand. Compromise and helpfulness don't work. One person, who turned out to be a first-class therapist, finally had a rage explosion when she worked with me. She hovered over me with a heavy chair ready to smash me. I calmly said: "Go ahead, I've lived my life," and she woke up from her trance.

Once I was called to a group to calm down a girl who attacked everyone in the group physically. The group members tried to hold her and to calm her down. In vain. Again and again she got up and fought. When I came in she charged with her head down into my belly and nearly knocked me over. Then I let her have it until I had her on the floor. Up she came again. And then a third time. I got her down again and said, gasping: "I've beaten up more than one bitch in my life." Then she got up, threw her arms around me: "Fritz, I love you." Apparently she finally got what, all her life, she was asking for.

And there are thousands of women like her in the States. Provoking and tantalizing, bitching, irritating their husbands and never getting their spanking. You don't have to be a Parisian prostitute to need that so as to respect your man. A Polish saying is: "My husband lost interest in me, he never beats me any more."

Once something happened that really scared me. Many patients "retroflect" their aggression and take it out on themselves, for instance by choking themselves. I used to let them choke *me* instead.

Until one day a girl meant business. I had not realized her schizoid personality. I had already begun to lose consciousness, when at the last moment I pushed my arms between hers and tore them apart. Since then I just give them my *arm* to choke. This is sometimes pretty painful too. There are quite a few stranglers in the world. With patients who have a good fantasy, a cushion will serve the purpose.

I myself have very little tendency to get violent without adequate provocation. I might get angry, and twice I have thrown people physically out of a seminar if they were unmanageably destructive and refused to leave. I hit back hard when attacked. I have a few times become violent with jealousy, but am mostly satisfied to torture my beloved with questions and relentless requests for detailed confessions.

As for the sex games, in the baths and otherwise, reticence does not apply to me. Freud would call me a polymorph pervert. I even learned to enjoy intimate kisses of some man friends. I used to enjoy screwing for hours, but now, at my age, I enjoy mostly being turned on without having to deliver the goods. I like my reputation as being both a dirty old man and a guru. Unfortunately the first is on the wane and the second ascending.

Once we had a party in the "big house" at Esalen. A beautiful girl was lying seductively on a couch. I sat next to her and said something like this: "Beware of me, I am a dirty old man." "And I,"

she replied, "am a dirty young girl." We had a short and delightful affair after that.

Mostly I feel good about this writing. I never expected this to be so easy. I begin to think about the possibility of writing a play—I don't imagine it yet. It's still very vague. And being a good actor and first-rate producer, I would do the whole thing as a "Fritz" production. Right now, quite a few people are crowding into this book, sneering at my letching, despising me for my lack of control, being shocked by my language, admiring me for my courage, confused by the multitude of contradictory features, desperate because they cannot pigeonhole me. I feel tempted to get into a dialogue, but. . .

The window is wide open. Faintly threatening murmur of the surf. Gentle blowing winds lift papers on the desk, too weak to make them fly. Like my soft beard stroking a maiden's face and breast and making them shiver with silent delight, making their nipples stand up in proud erection, patiently waiting to be lightly bitten.

My hands are strong and warm. A dirty old man's hands are cold and clammy. I have affection and love—too much of it. And if I comfort a girl in grief or distress and the sobbing subsides and she presses closer and the stroking gets out of rhythm and slides over the hips and over the breasts . . . where does the grief end and a perfume begin to turn your nostrils from dripping to smelling?

Those meetings and findings are like the temperature at Big Sur. Sure, we have no freezing and no overheat. But in between there is no indolence of sameness as on a tropical island. The cold is cold and shivery. The rain is wet and muddy. The sun burns the roof in the afternoon to suffocation. I have no extremes of relating. I don't kill and I don't sell out to a single-marriage situation. I have floating relationships, from the all-too-frequent kisses to loyalties of long standing.

The first kiss is a Rorschach Test
You touch a stranger's mouth and lips
You find a tightlipped "I don't care"
Or greediness that sucks you in
Indifference that's testing you
A peck that is dismissing you
A gentle warning: heed the hurt
A crunching maiming takes your breath
A stroking, sex-implying lick
A mouth that stinks like stomach shit
A dryness like frigidity
A tightness like a wrestler's arm
A foamy rubber flabbiness
A few that spell fulfillment:
A waiting, holding promises
For melting altogether.
Abolish the environment
In swooning isolation.
Each kiss, I say, is different
If you discover subtleties
With full alive involvement.

Die Engel die nennen es Himmelsfreud
Die Teufel die nennen es Höllenleid
Die Menschen die nennen es Liebe (H. Heine)
(The angels call it "Heaven's joy"
The devils, "Hellish torture"
Man calls it "love")

Esalen started out as an inn with the special attraction of the hot baths. When I came to Esalen it was still a public inn with a number of lectures and seminars starting, the bar and restaurant open to the public. The *innkeepers* were Mike Murphy and Dick Price. Now we are an expanding private institute with the *directors* Mike Murphy and Dick Price. Passing-by city slickers and indigent drug peddlers are eased out or thrown out. For a while, about a year ago, it was easy and natural to get LSD and marijuana here until Mike took a stand. Now we are proud to turn people on without drugs. We are said to produce instant cure, instant joy, and instant sensory awareness.

How the hell did we get into all this? Sure, there was in the beginning an intensity of longing for redemption and salvation. The mystic, the esoteric, the supernatural, the extrasensory perception seem to fit into the spirit of the place. Yoga-meditation to get to a higher level of existence seems to coincide with the dismay with the urban humdrum existence. The discarded soul was making a commercial re-entry.

The beauty of this was that they made a sincere attempt to get to the non-verbal level of their existence, but they did not realize that meditation, like analysis, is a trap. Like psychoanalysis it creates an imbalance, though on the opposite end of the scale.

These two imbalances could be compared with the defecation process. Constipation and diarrhea are opposite types of discharge, both interfering with the optimal function, (+) versus (−). In psychiatry we have the opposites of catatonic stupor (− excitement) and schizophrenia (+ excitement).

Meditation, neither shit nor get off the pot, seems to me an education towards catatonia, while the psychoanalytic technique of flight of ideas promotes schizophrenic thinking.

I have experienced both the quiet sitting in the Zendo and the verbiage production on the couch. Now both rest under their tombstones in my garbage bin.

I hate to use and acknowledge the word "normal" for the point of creative indifference. It is used far too often for the average and not for the point of optimal function.

I hate to use and acknowledge the word "perfect" for the point of creative indifference. It smells of achievement and praise.

I love to use and acknowledge the word *center*. It is the bull's-eye of the target. Such a target that hits the arrow every time.

I love all the imperfect meetings of target and arrow that miss the bull's-eye to the right and to the left, above and below. I love all the attempts that fail in a thousand ways. There is but one bull's-eye and a thousand good wills.

Friend, don't be a perfectionist. Perfectionism is a curse and a strain. For you tremble lest you miss the bull's-eye. You are perfect if you let be.

Friend, don't be afraid of mistakes. Mistakes are not sins. Mistakes are ways of doing something different, perhaps creatively new.

Friend, don't be sorry for your mistakes. Be proud of them. You had the courage to give something of yourself.

It takes years to be centered; it takes more years to understand and to be *now*.

Until then, beware of both extremes, perfectionism as well as instant cure, instant joy, instant sensory awareness.

Until then, beware of any helpers. Helpers are con-men who promise something for nothing. They spoil you and keep you dependent and immature.

It feels good to play preacher and enjoy a pompous Nietzsche style.

How did the target Esalen hit my arrow, poised towards it years before I knew of the target's existence?

In or about 1960 I practiced in Los Angeles. I was still smarting from a mess of two operations in Miami, tearing myself away from Marty, and taking too frequent LSD trips. Nothing really worthwhile occurred. In spite of Jim Simkin's support I could not get through to the profession and I could not get rid of a feeling of being condemned to life. I did not even have a depression. I was fed up with the whole psychiatric racket. I did not know what I wanted. Retirement? Vacation? Change of profession?

I decided on a trip from Los Angeles to New York, but the other way around—a world trip by boat.

I always loved going by boat as much as I disliked the crowded transport planes. Except the one time when, at the height of our love, Marty and I flew to Europe. Then sitting close together felt good.

Usually I am squeezed in by strangers who pester me with questions and need for attention. There I wait in my aircage and bless an occasional dozing off.

I love flying as much as I dislike being flown. In contrast to driving: I like as much being driven as I dislike driving myself.

That boat trip from Los Angeles to New York took fifteen months.

First stop, Honolulu, Hawaii. This was like a *déjà vu* of Miami Beach.

Before we sailed into the harbor, I had, perhaps, the greatest visual experience of my life.

When you fly into Los Angeles at night, you see squashed Christmas trees of tremendous size waiting for you. The glimmer and glitter makes you forget their phony neon stuff. It makes you forget that ugly smog cloud that greets your entry into the city of a hundred towns.

Now, multiply that multi-color glitter many times over and take a shower bath in it. This happened to me before Hawaii.

I love the silver sparkle of the firmament like everybody else. Now it was intensified by the clean ocean air and I was curious to see if I could get still more out of it. I took a small amount of LSD and then it happened.

Indescribable is a flat word. There was no distance, no two dimensions. Every star was closer or farther away, every one played a color dance like the planet Venus before it dips into the ocean. The universe, the void of all voids, for once was filled.

Then Japan—Tokyo and Kyoto. Impossible to describe the contrast of those two cities, merely a night of high-efficiency train service apart. In Tokyo, the people insensitive, unaware of each other, crowded in a way that, by comparison, sardines in a can have more *Lebensraum*. At least they don't bruise each other. Yet I had a peak experience: the loving eyes of an old woman, squatting in the gutter, polishing my shoes. I threw a cigarette stub away. Greedily she picked it up. Then I gave her my half-full packet. She turned her head towards me. Dark eyes melted and shone with love that made my knees weak. I still see those eyes occasionally. Impossible love made possible.

Only once before in my life did I see such love in somebody's eyes. Lotte Cielinsky, my first love. I had to play a French nobleman in a comedy. She came backstage and when she saw me in my costume and make-up her face underwent a transformation as if the heavens had opened just for her. Beautiful, most beautiful.

A Japanese doctor had designed a method of treating neuroses. Three days in bed. The patient is only allowed to get up to go to the john. Let's try this! Use it for smoking interruption! Young doctor, speaks no English. Non-medical assistant makes all arrangements. I ask for interpreter. Yes, but I have to pay extra.

Have a good room by myself. Perhaps the first European ever. The other patients stare at me like a queer animal. Doctor's wife brings the food, serves it on her knees. Passing the doctor's office on the second afternoon. Doctor sits rigidly in stunning habit, apparently waiting the whole day for me. Don't know the customs. Interpreter girl knows very very little English.

I stand it for over two days, then throw a temper tantrum, run out and buy cigarettes. Get the bill. Two hours of interpreter girl costs three times the price of three days in sanatorium. I don't feel cured.

A Japanese psychologist whom I had met in the States suggested a Zen Master, Roshi Ihiguru. Instant Zen. Satori in a week. No joke. M., another American psychologist, and I are his first European pupils. We, plus eight Japanese young men, make up the class. This is a great event. Press and photographers are called in. I've kept the newspaper clippings.

M. and I have a large room to ourselves. We have to spread and roll our mattresses for the night, because during the day the master has a few minutes personal audience with each pupil. During this audience I have to lie in a full-length prostrate position before him. He asks some cliché questions and I am dismissed for the day. He is a small pompous man with a rather high voice and takes himself and his work very seriously.

We get up at five o'clock in the morning and are supposed to "sit" in the famous lotus position with the famous leg distortions, practically the whole day. We two outsiders were soon allowed to have chairs. After two days the master introduced his specialty. "Exhale with a barking noise. Do this for a ??? time." What is between "do it for minutes" and "do it for hours"?

Food is astonishingly good. The master's wife puts herself out to supplement the Japanese dishes by some Western ones. At the end of each meal we pour tea into the bowl and use a slice of some vegetable to clean out the last grain of rice.

I think that the Japanese race has adjusted itself to the scarcity of food by shrinking and thus living comfortably on a low-calorie diet. When I walked in a crowd I felt like a giant among dwarfs and I am only 5 feet 9 inches tall.

In any case I did not starve, though I occasionally sneaked out for some smoke and chocolate.

I don't believe anyone got any enlightenment or *satori*, but the experience was interesting. When it came to paying, I got a shock. The price was ten dollars which included room, board and tuition for a whole week. When I was told that, I could not accept it and gave him thirty dollars which he accepted graciously and he did a brush painting for me with his wife throwing in a bonus of a sweetish flowerbit drawing.

I made one real booboo. On the third morning, I was told that the water for the bath was ready. There was a big barrel with steaming water about two feet wide and three feet deep. I did not quite know how to immerse myself, but managed to climb in and soap myself. I used the big ladle that was hanging next to the barrel to douse my head. The whole thing was uncomfortable but better than nothing.

Then I heard of my crime. The water was heated with great effort and was common property. The ladle served to take out water as you needed it for washing. I had spoiled the "bathing" for the whole class.

My belated apology. We are just too spoiled and take for granted what for other people is a hard-earned luxury.

I know what a *satori* experience is, though I have not made the total enlightenment grade, in case such a thing exists. *Siddhartha*, after all, is a product of Hermann Hesse's sincere fantasy.

One of the most surprising and spontaneous *satori* experiences happened about twelve years ago in Miami Beach.

I was walking down Alton Road, when I felt a transformation coming over me. At that time I did not know anything about, nor had I ever taken, a psychedelic drug. I felt my right side getting cramped and nearly paralyzed. I started limping, my face got slack, I felt like a village idiot, my intellect went numb and stopped functioning altogether. Like a thunderbolt the world jumped into existence, three-dimensional, full of color and life—definitely not with a depersonalization—like life-"less" clarity—but with a full feeling of: *"This is it, this is real."* This was a complete awakening, coming to my senses, or my senses coming to me, or my senses making sense.

I had, of course, known (mainly through dreams and reading Korzybski) of a non-verbal level of existence, but had regarded it as a substratum, rather than a real, the most real form of being.

　　In contrast to Tokyo, I fell in love with Kyoto. I fell so much in love with Kyoto that I seriously considered settling there. Gentle people regarding each other, looking openly, with respect. Once, in a cafe, I left a journal behind that I had finished. The proprietress ran two blocks after me to return it. Even the taxi-drivers were honest.

　　I sat for hours in the garden of my hotel watching ducks policing impudent and ancient carp, and arrogant swans who hardly craned their necks toward such goings-on.

　　Harmony and serenity in plenty, and not just the castle and the golden temple. A few times I found it even in a downtown strip-tease joint. One number that would have been obscene in any Western show became an artistic event. The actress portrayed a widow masturbating in front of her dead husband's shrine. She did this with so much devotion and beauty of movement that it conveyed the message of a love that kept the audience silent, not applauding.

　　And so to Zen. The place, I believe, was called the Daitokuji temple, one of hundreds of temples to be found in the north of Kyoto. The owner, an American, watched and presided over her husband's shrine, a library, and extensive writings. Once she had a herd of visitors and donned her impressive costume. Truly a high-priestess of Zen.

The students were a motley international group. Some of them led a simple life pretending to be Zen monks. I really liked them and their sincere striving for redemption. We met often in the evening before the "sitting." In the beginning, Mrs. Sasaki spoke about breathing and other Zen-related topics, but after four weeks she and her pupils became more and more interested in Gestalt Therapy. I gave as little as possible. I wanted to explore their position and the results of their work.

The Roshi was a rather young Zen monk who became very fond of me. Before I left Kyoto, I invited him and the crowd to an elaborate (and, I must admit, delicious) Chinese dinner that had twelve courses. I had learned that he badly wanted a wristwatch. After two days, I discovered he did not wear the watch I had given to him. I could not understand, because it was a good watch. Then I found out that he had put the watch with his most precious possessions in his shrine, his place of devotion.

Zen had attracted me as the possibility of a religion without a God. I was surprised to see that before each session we had to invoke and bow before a Buddha statue. Symbolism or not, to me it was again a *re*ification leading to a *de*ification.

"Sitting" was not a great strain, as we interrupted the two or three hour session with some walking. We had to breathe in a certain way and keep the attention on the breathing in order to minimize the intrusion of thoughts while the master was strutting up and down, occasionally correcting our posture. Each time he came close to me, I got anxious. This, of course, threw my breathing out of gear. He only hit me very few times. He had very strong stomach muscles which he liked to show off. I had the impression that his muscles mattered more to him than his enlightenment.

I was there for two months. There was not time to be properly introduced to the *koan* game. He only gave me one childishly simple *koan*: "What color is the wind" and he seemed to be satisfied when, as an answer, I blew in his face.

I am stuck again. I looked over the last two paragraphs and found them rather garbled and jumpy in parts. What will the editor do? For by now I see that this writing wants to become a book. That falsifies my original intentions to write only for myself, to sort myself out, to investigate my smoking and other remaining symptoms. It falsifies my honesty, too. Not only did I catch myself twice in the sin of omission, but, what's more, I began to hesitate to bring in living people. Fear of being sued, and that sort of thing. Well, *que será, será*. Whatever will be, will be, as Edith Piaf sings.

So far, this writing has already done a lot for me. My original boredom has changed into excitement. I am writing from three to six pages a day, between the seminars or at night. I am getting stingy with my time, and often prefer writing to going down to the lodge. I like to show parts of the manuscript to some friends and I am delighted by their response over and over. When Teddy, my secretary, comes in for doing correspondence or tidying up, she has first to read what I have written and to give me her judgement.

Through the mobilization of the writing excitement, I feel better throughout. I am getting and giving more and more love. The dirty old man gets somewhat cleaner. But what can I do if more and more beautiful young and not-so-young girls and frequently this or that man are hugging and kissing me?

My serenity, humor, and therapeutic skill are on the increase, as is my happiness. Interestingly, I feel in the last few years that I am no longer condemned to, but blessed with, life.

I am stuck because I don't know if I should now write about my dead friend Paul Weiss, who was an integral part of my growing interest in Zen, or if I should continue on my world trip. I notice that my writing gets smaller and smaller when I mention Paul. I felt indeed often small in his presence.

Paul, if I only could do more than just pull you out of my garbage bin. If I only could bring you back to life. You were solid and real, wise and cruel. Mostly exactingly cruel to yourself. Disciplining yourself with Zen-sitting and demanding clearest and honest thinking. Never compromising in essentials.

You were one of the few people in my life to whom I listened. Even if what you said seemed preposterous at the time, I always put your statement in my belly and let it ripen. Nearly always it bore fruit.

His remarks were not always critical. Once he gave me great support. I was trying to come to grips with Heidegger and Paul remarked: "What do you need Heidegger for? You've said it much better and more to the point."

Paul and Lotte had the most amazing marriage. He was a killer and she was indestructible. Lotte asked the most irritating questions with the sweetest smile, (Lotte is sweet and gentle and a good Viennese cook) and he pounced on her with violence and love.

I had met Lotte first after a paper I read to the Society for the Advancement of Psychotherapy, on "The Theory and Technique of Personality Integration." She came and worked with me. We became, and still are, very good friends.

Paul, who worked on cancer research, had a severe obsessional neurosis. He worked mostly with Lore, and became a very good and effective therapist, mainly for borderline cases. Apart from Gestalt Therapy, he became very involved with Zen, made several trips to Japan, and invited some Zen monks to come to this country. Lotte complained about this invasion of their well-kept house.

From then on, I became more and more fascinated with Zen, its wisdom, its potential, its non-moral attitude. Paul tried to integrate Gestalt and Zen. My endeavor accentuated more the creation of a viable method of opening up this kind of human self-transcendence to the Western man. In this I was encouraged by Aldous Huxley, who called *Gestalt Therapy* "the only psychotherapeutic book worth reading."

My visit to Japan was a failure as far as any achievement in Zen was concerned. It reinforced my conviction that, as in psychoanalysis, something must be wrong if it takes many years and decades to get nowhere. The best that can be said is that psychoanalysis breeds psychoanalysts and the study of Zen breeds Zen monks.

The value of both, the enlargement of awareness and the release of the human potential, is to be affirmed; the efficiency of both methods is to be denied. They cannot be efficient, because they are not centered in the polarities of contact and withdrawal, the rhythm of life.

Yesterday I did not feel like writing at all. I had given the first pages of this section to Kay for typing. I felt an emptiness after that, nothing to go by, nothing to fill the void of nothing.

> A thousand plastic flowers
> Don't make a desert bloom
> A thousand empty shadows
> Don't fill an empty room

Then last night, the groping started again. I was groping in different directions. More than memories and experiences, I want to salvage my Gestalt philosophy. I want to come across in a language that is understandable to everyone. I want to bring across a living theory which is exact without being rigid. I want, I want, I want. I, I, I, I.

What is "I?" A composition of introjects (as Freud suggested), a thing the neurologist can localize in the brain, the organizer of our actions, the captain of my soul? Nothing of that sort. A small child has no "I" yet. He talks of himself in the third person. Eskimos use the third person singular instead of "I." Certain South Sea tribes say "here" instead of "I."

We have seen that the biological gestalt which emerges as the transient organizer takes over the control of the total organism. Every organ, the senses, movements, thoughts, subordinate themselves to this emerging need and are quick to change loyalty and function as soon as that need is satisfied and then retreat into the background. As soon as the next need emerges, all the parts put themselves into its service and will, in a wholesome person, go all out for the completion of that gestalt. All the parts of the organism *identify* themselves temporarily with the emergent gestalt.

A similar process happens on the social level. In an emergency— a flood, an earthquake, a victory celebration—many people will identify themselves with it and will *part*icipate, will take part and join with others to attend and to contribute their share.

The "I" is the foreground figure experience. It is the sum of all emerging needs, the clearing house for their satisfaction. It is the constancy factor within the relativity of inner and outer demands. It is the responsibility agent for whatever it identifies itself with:

Response-able, capable of responding to the situation—not "responsible" in the moralistic sense of taking on obligations dictated by duty.

In the example of the water imbalance, the two statements "I am thirsty" and "I am not thirsty" are not logical contradictions, but identifications with the different states of dehydration or the absence of it.

O.K., so far so good. We recognize that "I" is not a static thing but a symbol for an identification function. However, we are by no means out of the woods. First of all, if Freud speaks of total introjection, he also means an identification process. If a girl has introjected her mother, so he says, she identifies herself so much with her mother that she behaves "as if" she were her mother.

Furthermore, the term "identification" is a descriptive term and tells us little of what is actually going on.

Finally, our term needs some more clarification: "identification with," "identification as," and "being identified with."

Now it looks as if we have to play some semantic fitting games. One of the aims of my philosophy is to be cohesive, that is, to be applicable to *all* occurring events, including the inorganic as well as the organic world. The more comprehensive the intellectual support is, the less wobbliness will be encountered in the higher, that is, the superimposed levels.

Since meeting Friedlander, I have learned the art of proper polarizing. The opposite of "identification with" is alienation. Self-alienation has become an important term in existential psychiatry.

"Identification as" has the opposite: confluence—distinction vs. undifferentiated background.

I have used the term confluence since 1940. I don't believe it has found its way into psychiatry yet. As a word, it is easy to grasp, as a term it is not easy at all. It is one of the *nothing* categories.

I am smoking. I am blowing a ring. I can identify this as a smoke ring. A gentle wind is stretching it. It is floating upward, distorting its shape, enlarging it, thinning it. It is still there—vaguely. It loses its boundaries. It's disappearing. I have to strain to be still aware of it. Now it is gone. Gone? No. It is there in *confluence* with the air and it is no longer identifiable. We would have to sample and analyze the air in the room to trace its substance, although its gestalt, its definition, is gone.

I am leaving the room. On returning, I smell the smoky air. I made *contact*. I am now aware of the smoky air.

In *confluence*, awareness is reduced to nothing. In *contact*, awareness is intense. Before I re-entered the room, I was *not aware* of the smoky air. I was *isolated, separated* from it. This phenomenon is the best known and best investigated in modern psychiatry: repression, block, inhibition, compartmentalization, scotoma, blind spot, blank, amnesia, wall, censor, plastic sheet, etc. The recovery of the hidden treasure is the purpose of psychoanalytic technique.

As soon as I remove the separating instance, I am in contact with the hidden phenomenon. I am in touch.

I have to go carefully, step by step, to stay consistent. No wonder that at present the writing is not flowing. Neither do I expect that the reading will be easy. I used to say that the films I am making will be my testament, but now this book is moving more into the foreground and the film-making has lost much of its excitement. The four-week workshop is ending tomorrow and it looks as if we have much interesting film material for bringing Gestalt Therapy across, but the thrill and full involvement which I felt when I started with videotapes and movie-making has diminished. We have at least two films on confluence, many on contact functions and *recovery*, and also some on *un*covering.

The zero point here is *dis*covery. Any discovery is accompanied by an "aha!" experience, a pleasant or unpleasant shock of varying intensity. I maintain that learning is *un*covering of something "new," for instance, realizing that something is possible. The removal of a block is *recovery* of something "old," something that belongs to us, something we have alienated, denied its rightfully belonging to us.

While current therapy is satisfied with *recovery* as the antidote to the impoverishment brought about by repression, etc., Gestalt Therapy is still more interested in the *un*covering of an individual's dormant potential.

What's more, in spite of its usefulness, the whole repression theory and therapy has to be re-examined.

Topdog: Stop, Fritz, what are you doing?
Underdog: What do you mean?
Topdog: You know very well what I mean. You're drifting

from one thing to another. You are starting something like identification, then mention confluence. Now I already see that you are ready to plunge into a discussion on repression.

Underdog: I still don't see your objection.

Topdog: You don't see my objection? Man, who the hell can get a clear picture of your therapy?

Underdog: You mean I should take a blackboard and make tables and categorize every term, every opposite neatly?

Topdog: That's not a bad idea. You could do that.

Underdog: No, I won't. At least not at this stage. But I tell you what I can do. I can eventually use different typefaces for biographical, philosophical, therapeutic, and poetic material.

Topdog: Well, that's at least an idea.

Underdog: So what do you want me to do? Stop letting the river flow? Stop playing my garbage bin game?

Topdog: Well, that wouldn't be a bad idea, if you would sit down and discipline youself like Paul did and write:

    1) your biography
    2) your theory
    3) case histories, dream work, etc.
    4) poetry, if you must

Underdog: Go to hell. You know me better. If I try to do something deliberate and under pressure, I get spiteful and go on strike. All my life I have been a drifter. . .

So let me drift and sail the seas
Of hundred verbal oceans
And let such captain be in charge
As is a top controller.

So let me sleep as long I like
And have a lazy breakfast
Then brave a wind that's shivering me
The waves, the boat, and friends aboard.

So let me travel by myself
Without a wife and children
Without a guru or a friend
And any obligation.

So let me empty all my trunks
Get rid of surplus baggage
Until I'm freed of all that crap
That clutters up my living.

So let me be and die my way
A clearing house for people
A lonely bum who loves to joke
And think and play, and is all there.

So let the world, the cell, the bees
Be filled with thought-emotions
And let me drift and sail the seas
Of hundred verbal oceans.

Topdog:
    I hear your plea
    I feel your tears.
    Farewell, you lonely sailor.

You made your bed
You forged your chains.
Enjoy your heavy dancing.

Farewell for now
But I'll be back
With my relentless bugging.

Until the last day of your life
When we will part forever.
You married me, and not your wife
And you thought you were clever.

For you is I and I is you
And we will die together.

First reader: Hey there, stop that sentimental stuff. I paid my fee to get a peep of what you have been doing. You left Japan and went from there—where?

Fritz: To Hong Kong, of course.

Second reader: Got quite a few bargains there, didn't you?

Fritz: Yes and no. I got a woolen overcoat that cost only $30, but it was skimpily made. I got a white dinner jacket which I used on board, but it has been hanging unused for years now in my closet.

Third reader: What was the political situation like?

Fritz: I don't remember. I went for kicks out to the barbed wire that separates the Crown Colony from China, just to be able to say that I had a peep into Red China.

Third reader, again: There were many refugees from Red China?

Fritz: Yes, they were living in terribly over-crowded lean-tos on hills and in over-overcrowded apartment buildings. Hey, you guys, what are you doing to me? Asking questions like journalists, treating me like a VIP who has answers to dole out—

Readers, together: Pipe down, Fritz. Firstly, we are a figment of your imagination. And it is you who think you are a VIP.

Fritz: Well, well, I admit all this. You want me to seize the opportunity to talk about projections?

Readers: No, no. We want you to go on with your world trip. You said the arrow was poised to hit the target—Esalen—long before you went there, and this had to do with your trip around the world.

Fritz: That's right. In spite of my restless gypsy nature, I was looking for a place to put up my tent for a considerable time. Kyoto, with its gentle people, seemed to be one possibility. The other was Elath, in Israel.

Readers: Aha, the old Jew's homecoming to the land of his ancestors. And we thought you were an atheist.

Fritz: That's correct. Although I had at least one religious experience in my life, in 1916 in the trenches of Flanders.

I was a medic attached to the 36th Pioneer batallion. This was the unit especially trained for attacking the enemy with poison gas. My original order to stay with the medical officer in the third trench was changed and I had to go to the more dangerous front trench. We were supported by two companies of poison gas mine-throwers. At three o'clock a.m., we made the gas attack, and within minutes we got the full barrage of the British guns. Two hours of hell, and yet I did not have many casualties to attend to. I myself got a superficial wound on my forehead, which is still visible except when my face is tanned and looks in some photos like a third eye. Later I learned that the third trench medical dugout had received a direct hit and the doctor and his two medics were killed.

On our march back, a stunningly beautiful sunrise. I felt the presence of God. Or was it gratitude, or the contrast between the gunfire and a serene silence? Who can tell?

In any case, it was not enough to convert me into a believer. Perhaps Goethe is right when Faust answers Marguerite:

> Religious is a man
> who is involved in art
> or also if he can
> rely on science smart.
> But failing such support,
> a man who has as lot
> a void he can't afford—
> such man needs faith in God.

This is badly translated. Goethe is the one poet whom nobody can translate. He has a unity of language, rhythm, and meaning which loses its subtlety as soon as one makes him speak another language.

No, mine was not a Jew's homecoming, though for a while I played sincerely with the idea of making my home in Israel. But for my sake, not for the land and its people.

My relation to Judaism and the Jews is extremely undefined. I know quite a bit about German, Greek, and Roman history. About the history of—I can't even say my people, so little am I identified with them—the Jewish people, I know next to nothing. The East-European Jews with the caftans and *payes* (long whisker curls) that I saw in my youth were uncanny, frightening, like monks, not belonging to my world. Yet I love Jewish stories and their pregnant wit. Israelis come frequently to my seminars, and especially if they are *Sabra* (born in Israel), I am prejudiced in their favor. I have veneration and appreciation for the wholesome Jew who is one with his religion, history, and way of life. Their Zionism makes sense, though I looked and still look upon Zionism as an unrealistic, foolish sentimentality. The majority of Jews did not come to Israel in the spirit. They came as refugees from Hitler, and there are many places in the world where Jewish ingenuity could have made deserts bloom more easily, and with less dissemination of hostility. In the balance, however, I bow to you, Israel, and your Makabbi spirit. You have given much respect to the Jews in the world. Even the American anti-Semitism has greatly diminished. To be a Jew no longer disqualifies one automatically from a job for which he is fit. As for the latent American Fascism, the target will be the Negro and the hippie rather than the Jew, and the Negro will not suffer it as submissively, with cowardice, as the European Jew did. He has tasted freedom, and flexes his muscles.

Like anything else, this writing is dictated by the rhythm of contact and withdrawal. After I wrote the last page, I felt a pressure in my head and tiredness. Now tiredness is the organismic signal par excellence for withdrawing. Again, I feel the same tiredness after only two sentences. . .

I went back to the couch to get in touch with the pressure and came up with *coping*, which is a much more appropriate polarity to withdrawal. Contact is present in both situations. To over-simplify: Coping is being in touch with the OZ (outer zone, otherness, environment); withdrawing is getting in touch with the MZ (middle zone), or even with the SZ (inner or self zone). Regression is not a neurotic symptom as Freud saw it. And it certainly is not the outstanding characteristic of a neurotic. On the contrary, withdrawing, regression, and retreat mean taking up a position in which we can cope, or from which we get needed support, or in order to attend to a more important unfinished situation.

If the elasticity of the figure/ground formation is impaired, if, in our case, coping and withdrawing don't supplement each other, we have to deal with *chronic* coping and *chronic* withdrawal, both symptoms of pathology. Chronic coping is known as fixation, hanging on, compulsiveness, phoniness, etc. Chronic withdrawal is known as being "out of touch," shut off, and in extreme cases, as catatonic stupor.

If a battalion is in a difficult situation, threatened with annihilation, loss of men and ammunition, it will engage in a "strategic withdrawal." It will withdraw to a more secure position and will acquire support of men and ammunition, maybe even moral support, until the *in*complete gestalt is completed and it again has adequate manpower, hardware, and fighting spirit.

There is the story of the two analysts. The young one, exhausted in the evening, asks his senior colleague, "How can you stand it to listen the whole day to all those associations?" He answers, "Who listens?"

Here again we have the two extremes of hanging on—chronic coping, often called "grim determination"—and shutting off one's ears. Hanging on would lead to the annihilation of the battalion, and it leads to the exhaustion of the junior analyst.

A banker in the days of the black Friday who identifies his existence exclusively with being a moneymaker, holding on to that image, incapable of coping with the market, has no other choice than to commit suicide.

A person who feels impotent to cope with the situation at hand, who will not let go, will often use the most primitive of all means of coping—killing. In other words, killing and violence are symptoms of chronic coping.

In April, 1933, after the Nazis had taken over, I went to Aitingon, who was the president of the Berlin psychoanalytic association, and told him that I saw warnings on the wall. He said, "You are not reality-oriented. You are running away." So I did. My reality was my impotence to cope with Hitler's SS. It took him two more years to get re-oriented and to go to Palestine.

Many Jews could have been saved during the Hitler regime if they could have let go of their possessions, relatives, and fear of the unknown.

Many could have been saved if they could have overcome their inertia and foolish optimism.

Many could have been saved if they would have mobilized their own resources instead of waiting for someone to rescue them.

If, if, if.

I woke up this morning dazed and heavy. Sitting on my bed, numbed and in a trance, as I have seen inmates of mental hospitals withdraw into their ruminations. Ghosts, Hitler's victims, mostly my and Lore's relations, visiting me, pointing their fingers: "You could have saved me," bent on making me feel guilty and responsible for them.

But I am holding onto my credo: "I am responsible only for myself. You are responsible for yourselves. I resent your demands on me, as I resent any intrusion into my way of being."

I know I am holding on just a bit too tight.

I feel frustrated and know at the same time that "I" frustrate "myself." The target, Esalen, seems to move further and further away. Even Elath, where (besides Kyoto) I saw the other possibility of settling, seems out of reach.

Yet I feel real and content. I am in touch with all three zones. I know I am sitting at my desk. I feel the pen sliding over the paper, I see my cluttered desk. The lamp above me casts the shadow of my hand over the forming words.

I am also in touch with my inner zone, the feeling of contentment, tiredness after a day's negotiation with a commission from Washington, D.C. about a grant for the coming "blowout" center, an eagerness to go on with the book.

I am also in touch with the middle zone, often called the mind. In this zone, I imagine, I talk subvocally, often called thinking; I remember, plan, rehearse. I know that I am imagining, conjuring up past events. I know they are not real, but images. If I thought that they were real, I would be hallucinating, that is, incapable of distinguishing reality from fantasy. This is the main symptom of a psychosis.

A sane person, in playing games, in going through past events, in daydreaming of future fulfillments and catastrophes, *knows* that he is in an "as if" state from which he can quickly return to the actual reality.

There is one exception, which in a deeper sense is not an exception—the dream. Any dream has the quality of being real. Any dream is a hallucination. Any dream feels natural. One is not aware of the often extreme absurdity of situations and events.

Any dream appears to be real and this is justified because the dream *is* a reality. It is an existential message, though coded in cryptic language.

Any dream is a spontaneous event. Fantasy, by contrast, can be deliberate to a very great degree. There seems to be no limit to fantasizing, provided we don't check it out and compare with the limiting possibilities of reality.

To go to Elath now would involve a lot of planning, time, money, cancelling of engagements, etc.

To go there in fantasy is easy, providing I have not blotted out my memory. When I go there, or, as I like to call it, when I take my time machine, I find myself halfway between Bersheika and Elath. Some ruins, a refreshment station, and a gas pump.

I fill up my VW which I picked up in Germany a few months before. The idea of having to explain this delivery is disturbing, interfering with the interesting situation in the half-way place. The fact is that I drove those 500 kilometers through the desert by myself and I doubt if I would have dared to do that except in an aircooled car like the VW.

Contrary to my expectations, the drive through the desert was not boring at all. The road was very small, but macademized and for the most part in good repair. Except for some Bedouins with their camels and tents, I did not meet any people, though I saw a kibbutz and a military camp from a distance. Elath was a disappointment—more tin shanties than houses, dusty and very warm. And this was winter. I very well could believe the stories of how unbearably hot it would be in summertime.

I checked into a hotel behind the posh Elath Hotel. I hate the chrome-plated hotels where one is waited on all the time. I often feel somewhat paranoid in small, elegant hotels; the vulture-like bellboys and elevator boys and chambermaids hover over me and are ingratiating and nice in return for a tip.

The whole scene seemed drab, and I decided to go back, within a couple of days, to Ein Hod, an art colony, where I felt comfortable. But. . .

There were beachcombers, and the land, and the seascape.

Instead of sticking to that resolve, I stayed for over four weeks. There was no love affair, no cultural attractions; the beach was stony rather than beautifully sandy as in Haifa, but. . .

I found the beachcombers, mostly Americans, fascinating.

Today we call them hippies and find them by the thousands. Sure, among our bohemian crowd in Berlin there was an occasional character who made a profession of doing nothing, but the majority were eager beavers to become important and make something out of their lives, and very many did.

I had also met beatniks who had tried and given up; angry people hitting their heads against the iron rules of society.

I had met Zen students a few months before who had given up without anger and were busy finding redemption.

To find the beachcombers here was an event.

To find people who were happy just to be, without goals and achievements.

To find them, of all countries, in Israel, where each and all were straining to build a lasting homestead.

To find people who were not even busy vacationing—you know that business of tanning, greasing your skin, wearing dark glasses, going to cocktail parties, gossiping about figures on the beach, talking about dieting and prices and attempts to give up smoking.

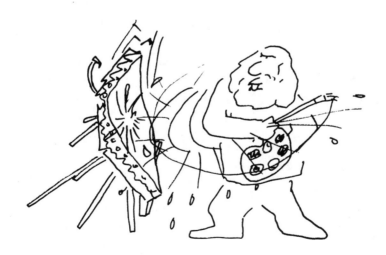

Now and then I used one of the beachcombers as a model for my painting. Painting had become my preoccupation in Israel. Until Elath, I had never painted with so much enthusiasm and involvement. Painters like Van Gogh were stimulated and in search of landscapes. Lost spinsters are in search of "subjects." Here was living color; here where the Negev muzzles the Red Sea, flanked by the mountains of Jordan and Egypt; here where the sun stirs up color after color from the heights of the mountains and penetrates to the underwater life of corals and gorgeously colored fishes; here eyes could feast on colors and shapes varying every hour of the day.

In the depth of the Red Sea there was an eel-like creature, about four to five feet long and at least one foot wide, a living sculpture in orange and carmine. A wave? A magic carpet? Joyful serenity actualized? I saw it only once, though I went after him a few times in a glass-bottomed boat.

I did not dare to paint those mountains, but I finally had enough courage to indulge in portraits. The porter from our motel liked to sit for me. I still have two of his pictures. I did some watercolor portraits, too. With oil paints I could always cheat and overpaint, but with watercolors I had to commit myself to subtle statements.

My earliest memory about painting is a visit to the Berlin National Gallery. I must have been about eight when my mother took me there. I was fascinated by the pictures of naked women; my mother was embarrassed about them and blushed. I recognized the religious pictures for what they were: propaganda for Jesus Christ. Some pictures struck me as beautiful—a large Raphael blue madonna with cute baby angels, and Rembrandt's "Man in a Golden Helmet." In school, drawing was one of my best subjects. Even at times when I went on strike in all other subjects, I liked the drawing class. No, there was one other exception—mathematics, which fascinated me so that I could not resist participation.

As usual, I did not prepare for school. I was already too involved in my attempt to become an actor. I was called to the blackboard to solve a difficult problem. I looked at it and succeeded, whereupon the professor remarked: "This is not the way I showed it yesterday. I give you an excellent in skill, and a demerit in diligence." I was impressed.

Drawing was always the copying of things—shading, perspective. It stayed so for a long time. My art appreciation was poor, mostly dictated by the fame of the painter. It took me a long time to see Picasso as the butcher he is, Gaugin as a poster producer, Rousseau as a "thingificator." Some painters grew in my appreciation—Klee, Van Gogh, Michelangelo, and Rembrandt, With Klee, I feel a growing fondness. Van Gogh's wildness fascinated and floored me. Michelangelo's ceiling of the Sistine chapel is like a beloved near relative whom I cherish with unwavering loyalty. But Rembrandt, to me, is like Goethe—a unified self—a transcending center overflowing with intense vitality. Once I sat for over an hour in front of his "Nightwatch" in the Reicksmuseum in Amsterdam.

Sometimes I have a craving for a picture, and then I have to buy it. Of course, this is not always possible. The painter might be famous and I am neither a rich man nor an art collector.

Of course, "if" I had been greedy and smart, I could have bought pictures for the $500 that I had earned in Bremerhaven, but then I might not have wanted to leave them behind and would have ended up in a concentration camp, or the pictures would have been burned as degenerate art. So we are back to, "If my aunt had wheels, she would be a motor car."

I started to take painting more seriously after I came to the States. The open-air life and sports of South Africa seemed to vanish in New York, the city of stone, haste, and culture. Lore did some writing, poetry and short stories. And she had her piano. She is a good pianist and in her youth it was touch and go whether she would go in for studying law and later psychology, or become a concert pianist.

I became a professional slave on the hour, by the hour, except for the long summer vacations, in Provincetown, Cape Cod.

We went there every summer and Lore still does. For me, the place was spoiled after "they" took the place's innocence and gave ugliness as payment. Actually, I am over-exaggerating.

The summer population was fishermen, artists, and psychoanalysts. I soon got busy with sailing and painting. Like with flying, I preferred to go sailing solo. Like with flying, I loved the great silence after turning off the motor and gliding down to earth.

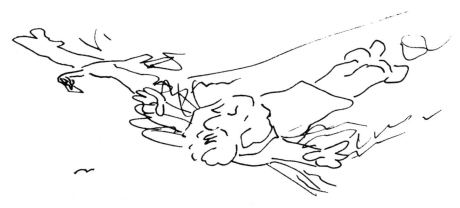

I never took to fishing and only caught some small fry and one flounder.

Painting became intense involvement, vaguely approaching an obsession. Soon I had one teacher after another. In Ein Hod, Israel, I did likewise.

I like a classroom atmosphere, with pupils jealously competitive and proud of their productions. I like the sinking into the isolation that accompanies the object-painter-canvas relationship. I like this forerunner of encounter groups, with the mutual praising and criticizing of each other's "masterworks." I like the fact that the canvas is the one place where you can commit any crime without being punished.

I liked nearly all my teachers, with their stereotyped saying: "All I want you to do is to express yourself," concealing the second part of the sentence, "as long as you do it my way."

I did not really become a painter until a few years ago. I had learned a lot of gimmicks, techniques, composition, color mixing. This all contributed merely to the reinforcement of the synthetic Fritz, the deliberate, computerizing, scanning approach to life. Only rarely did I achieve anything approaching the reality of self projecting itself on the canvas.

Sure, I sold some pictures; many hang on my walls now. Many can easily compete with the average American painter who wants to be different from his fellow painters and only exhibits the same boring identity of a need to be different, to have his own gimmick which he can then call style.

Then a few years ago, "it" clicked with a few watercolors. One day—mañana—I will paint again.

In a way, I compare this with my present writing, which suddenly, after so many decades, clicked. In both cases, painting and writing, I know that I have overcome the status of an amateur and have progressed from a symptom to an avocation.

Finally I returned to the States, still dragging my dismay with my profession as a heavy burden on my hunched shoulders. There was a meeting of the American Academy of Psychotherapists with three events that stand out. I was heartsick and had an angina pectoris attack that was rather disturbing and kept me in bed for a day.

The second was the beginning of a friendship with beautiful, wilful, and powerful Irma Shepherd—bright, warm, stubborn, and afraid of her vitality.

The third was an outburst of despair I had during a group session. That outburst was for real. Violent sobbing, not minding the presence of strangers, *de profundis*. This outburst did it. Afterwards I was able to re-assess my position and was willing to take up my profession again.

In writing this down, I made a *discovery*: I left out despair in my neurosis theory. For once, I want to make a table. The five layers of the neurosis are not strictly separated, but as a guideline to understanding, such an overview is useful:

a) the cliché layer
b) roles and games
c) implosion

d) impasse and explosion

e) authenticity

Clichés are both rigid and they are a testing ground—How are you? Nice weather. Handshake. Nodding the head. This simply indicates acknowledgement of another person's existence. It does not mean acceptance, though a deliberate withholding indicates affront. I am testing the other. Is he going to enter into a discussion about the weather or another neutral topic? Can we go on from there to slightly more precarious ground?

In doing so, we enter the game- and role-playing layer. We can call this layer the Eric Berne or Sigmund Freud domain. Preference is given to the "more than you" games: "My car is newer than yours," "My misery is more pitiful than yours." The number of games is more limited than the roles, though the latter are relatively few within the Freudian category: papa, mama, witch, baby, etc. Berne seems to have an affinity with the Freudian roles, but also with ugly frogs which become princes.

Most roles are means of manipulation—the bully, the helpless, the polite, the seducer, the good boy, the stroker, the wheedler, the Jewish mother, the hypnotist, the bore, etc., etc. They all want to influence you one way or another. Inanimate roles are rather frequent too—the iceberg, ball of fire, bulldozer, jelly, rock of Gibraltar, etc.

This afternoon I had a filmed dialogue with an Indian swami, Maharishi. His thing was a rather stereotyped getting in touch with the "infinite" to develop one's highest potential. As he played deaf or, at best, gave me a cackle that probably meant to be a laugh, I could not find out what that potential was, and how his meditation compares with our simpler coping/withdrawing technique. Still, he has good eyes and beautiful hands. I personally think he is a drag and I would not care to play a saint for all the fame and money in the world. His game and role is frozen, though I suspect that there must be situations where he would be capable of other roles.

Sometimes you find people on the other side of the scale. Helene Deutsch called them the "as if" type; people who have a hundred roles in their repertoire.

The classical example of limited role-playing is Dr. Jekyll and Mr. Hyde or the three faces of Eve. Both cases are already beyond the "as if" behavior. Both cases show a real dissociation. Both cases are different from the average dichotomy, for instance of a bank clerk who plays the ass-licker in the office and a tyrant at home.

Jerry Greenwald sent me a monograph which belongs somehow to our theme. He distinguishes two types of people: T people and N people. T stands for toxic, and N for nourishing. I can verify his findings, though I see other forms of destructiveness as well. An understanding of the coping/withdrawal rhythm can save you lots of strain; an understanding of T and N can greatly improve your vitality and might even save you quite a bit of unhappiness. All you need is some interest in this phenomenon.

The exception would be if you are a T-type yourself, and even then you might find someone who is more poisonous than yourself.

The first thing is to find extremes of T and N. What kind of people or situations leave you with exhaustion and irritation, and which with satisfacation and glowing? Which ones give you a sugar-coated dose of poison? Pay special attention to questions, advice-givers, drivers-crazy, shrill or somniforous voices.

Once you have confidence, watch each sentence, tone of voice, mannerisms. Extreme cases—stuttering, grimacing. What makes you uncomfortable? Do you have the compulsion to answer *every* question?

An excellent game can be played among close acquaintances. Watch and examine for a couple of days every sentence and all other forms of behavior. Once it "clicks" you will never lose the instinct for preferring N people to T types.

Arthur Schnitzler says in his *Paracelsus*: "We are always playing, but only the wise ones know it."

It is true. We often have to play roles—for instance to be deliberately on your best behavior—but the compulsive, manipulative, role-playing that replaces honest self-expression can and has to be overcome if you want to grow up.

The extreme poles of role-playing are avocation and pretending.

In the first case, you use the role as a vehicle to bring your essence across. You are supported by your skill, geniune feelings, and sensitivity. You are an N type.

In pretending, you lack this self-involvment. You fake an emotion that is not there, you lack the confidence in your ability. In short, you are a phony.

From the psychiatrist's point of view, the most important and interesting roles are introjected ones. Freud does not distinguish between introjection and copying, which is a learning process.

An introject is a dybbuk. Someone is possessing the patient and exists through him. The dybbuk is, like any true introject, a foreign body in the patient. Instead of being in the outer zone, as a person that can be encountered, he occupies a large part of the middle zone. The patient, instead of being self-regulated, being in tune with this figure/ground dominance, is being controlled by the needs and requirements of the dybbuk. He cannot come into his own until the dybbuk has been exorcised.

I found an extreme case of a dybbuk about ten years ago, during an American Psychological Association congress in San

Francisco. One of the members of a workshop group had a deadly wax-face. He looked like an encephalitis case, but without the symptoms of a damaged red nucleus. His whole behavior and smell conveyed to me the atmosphere of a corpse. I am used to relying on my often uncanny intuition, and asked him about a beloved person whom he had lost. And, true enough, there was a sudden death, there had been no mourning labor—to use an excellent term of Freud's—no tears and "goodbye," no separation, no burial. That person continued his existence, not, as so often is true, in character features, mannerisms, and way of thinking, but as a corpse.

I made him encounter his dybbuk, mobilize his grief, and say goodbye to it. We could not, of course, complete his mourning labor in the one session, achieve full closure, milk the symptom dry, but he became more lively, though not fully alive. His cheek lost its waxiness though it did not get a healthy color yet, and his walk became more elastic though he was not yet ready to dance.

One of the psychologists who attended that group was Wilson van Dusen, an existentialist. He suggested coming out to the west coast and doing some work at the Mendocino State Hospital. I welcomed this suggestion. I wanted to leave Miami. Marty rejected the idea of my marrying her. I was too old. She did not want to give up the security of her marriage and to imperil the pseudo-security of her children.

I took an apartment in San Francisco. Two of my hangers-on followed me; otherwise I had not much of a practice. I did my thing in the hospital and did not mind driving a hundred miles through the beautiful redwood country. There I became fond of Paul, a psychiatrist who loved farming and rearing children. I believe he has eleven of them by now. We played quite a number of exciting chess games.

At first, I was close to Wilson. We respected each other. I liked his children, was often an overnight guest in his house. Occasionally I rode on the pillion seat of his motorbike. In my youth, I had owned two motorbikes myself, but the pillion seat at my age (I was then about 65) was something different. At first I was afraid and tense, but soon I could let go and enjoy the rides. Once (I don't remember the occasion) his wife threw something at me and she smashed my wristwatch.

During my hospital work, I got acquainted with LSD and went quite frequently on trips, not aware that slowly I became quite paranoid and irritable. Anyhow, Wilson and I got quite estranged and I soon moved to Los Angeles. I saw him recently again and after a few days he thawed and we again felt good and warm towards each other.

One of his contributions is the discovery that the schizophrenic patient has holes in his personality. In the same paper, he mentions that existential psychiatry and theory lacks a practical and appropriate technique and that my approach provided that. Later on I followed up his idea of the holes and found that the same applies to the neurotic. One neurotic has no eyes, many have no ears, others no heart or memory or legs to stand on. Most neurotic people have no center.

Actually, this thesis is a follow-up of Freud's limited notion that the neurotic has no memory. Instead of memory, he has a blank or amnesia. Freud blames this amnesia not only for the patient's incomplete development, but also for his "acting out."

Wilson and I claim that there are many more holes which are responsible for the patient's incompleteness. A person can have a good memory, but no confidence or soul or ears, etc. Those holes can disappear, not by filling them with "overcompensations," but by changing the sterile void into a fertile void. The ability to do this depends again on the understanding of *nothingness*. The sterile void is experienced as *nothing*, the fertile void as *something* emerging.

In my youth, I took up Freud as my ready-made savior. I was convinced that I had damaged my memory through masturbation, and Freud's system centered around both sex and memory. I was also convinced that psychoanalysis was the only means of a cure.

We called a person who promised a cure without delivering the

goods a charlatan. Freud was a sincere scientist, a brilliant writer and discoverer of many secrets of the "mind." None of us, probably with the exception of Freud himself, realized the prematurity of applying psychoanalysis to treatment; none of us saw psychoanalysis in its proper context. We did not see it for what it actually was: a *research project*.

Today we spend years and millions on testing the safety and efficiency of every drug that comes on the market. This has not been done much with psychoanalysis, albeit there were or are no tests, or that the analysts themselves were or are phobic about putting their method to test. The government is very strict about drugs; the different states are very strict about licensing practitioners of psychotherapy; yet psychoanalysis in all its forms and names has escaped official scrutiny through an unformulated grandfather clause.

A neurologist complained to me about his bad memory. I found out that he was not able to recall instances over a span of three years. These three years coincided with the time of an unhappy marriage.

Now here is the decisive point. The repression was not the *cause* of his amnesia, but the *means whereby* he effected his phobic attitude towards the painful memory. To make sure, he had to blot out everything that happened during those three years. Now, Freud would agree with me that the recovery is not enough, although he also maintained that integration takes care of itself. In this case, he would say that the patient has to "work through" his situation.

Of course, as long as the patient blocks his memories he keeps the gestalt incomplete. If he is willing to go through the pain of his unhappiness and despair, he will come to a closure; he will come to terms with his resentments and will repair his memory, including all experiences which are not directly connected with the unhappy marriage.

Lore, like Goethe, has an eidetic memory. Eidetic people just have to close their eyes and look at their pictures, which tell the story with photographic exactness. I can get this kind of memory with psilocybin, a psychedelic mushroom drug.

Most people have it before falling asleep. I have it only after motor car rides or similar experiences. Most of my visual memory is in a fog, and my hypnogogic hallucinations (images before falling asleep) are still mostly of schizophrenic nature. They are in a cryptic language, like dreams, and disappear as soon as I try to catch them with my awake intellect. I suspect that this fog and my smoking are interrelated. Apart from idle speculations, I have so far not done anything about it, but I know that I will solve that problem too. Already since starting to write this book, three things have happened.

Firstly, the original boredom, the prime mover for writing, has turned into excitement. Then, I see much more and better. Much of the excitement that went into the motoric system (acting out), like masturbation and aggressing people, was not flowing into the sensory system. I am now more and more content to look and listen.

Finally, I noticed during the last months increased spells of tiredness. As a therapist, I used to withdraw into a half sleep, and rarely into a full sleep, whenever a patient drowned me with a hypnotic voice or was not in touch with me. Lately I have withdrawn somewhat less, stayed more in the middle ground, and very lately I am staying in touch with the tiredness *and* the world. Both integrate into a much more acute listening than before.

As far as my memory deficiency in my puberty years is concerned, it actually did not exist. I made the same mistakes as I did so often later. I blamed myself when I should have resented somebody else. I had a bad memory for learning dates in history and words in Latin. Both were torn out of context, strange, unfamiliar things. In other words, my bad memory was actually a good thing. To learn these words, etc., would be drill and repetition; that is, artifacts. I have shown that within a meaningful context I have no difficulties in absorbing material of interest. I gave as an example the way I learned English. My vocabulary is not tremendous, but adequate and to the point.

The situation in Los Angeles was not difficult at all. I had been there once before, in 1950. There was already a sprinkling of interest in professional circles. Jim Simkin had established himself as the first Gestalt Therapist in California.

Jim's interest in the Gestalt approach dates back to his college days. He had trained in New York with me and Laura (Lore has Americanized her name). Now, being off training, and meeting me much more in a social and co-professional context, a number of difficulties were revealed. He was square, uptight, over-exact, with a great love for a small inner circle. He and Ann, his wife, have a strong Jewish background and are still involved in Judaism. I know he respected my genius and despised my sloppiness and easy-going ways. As the years went by, he became much more spontaneous and open and used his exactness for his specific and successful style in Gestalt Therapy. We finally became good and trusting friends.

The interest in my work increased, but I did not feel accepted. Even professionals who worked with me successfully were careful not to identify themselves with Gestalt Therapy, or with that crazy guy, Fritz Perls.

In one of my groups there was a guy who was involved in a number of "far out" things—yoga, massage, therapy, Charlotte Selver's sensory awareness. His name is Bernie Gunther. He is a good *entrepreneur*—not very creative, but capable of synthesizing and putting to good use what he takes from different souces. He, like Bill Schutz, certainly turns people on. I have little doubt that he will climb up the ladder to the top.

He arranged some lectures for me in Los Angeles. I was amazed that there was an overflow attendance. I had not realized that Gestalt Therapy had begun to take root.

Christmas 1963, he suggested my participation in a workshop at a place in mid-California, called Esalen.

The target Esalen scored a bull's-eye with the arrow Fritz Perls. A landscape comparable to Elath; beautiful people on the staff as in Kyoto. An opportunity to teach. The gypsy found a home and soon a house.

He found something else as well. A respite for a sick heart.

Modern man lives and moves between the extreme poles of concreteness and abstractions.

We usually understand by the word concreteness those things, facts, and processes which in principle are accessible to everybody, which belong to everybody's *Umwelt*—environment, personal world, the zone of *otherness*, the *outer* zone.

If we have two or more people together, then their personal worlds will, to a large extent, coincide; the *Umwelt* becomes a *Mitwelt*—a common world, shared environment. On the surface, they deal with and identify the same facts and things.

As soon as we look a little bit deeper, we recognize the fallacy of this over-simplification, because many things and facts have very different meanings for each one of us, depending on our specific interests and needs for completing the unfinished situation of each individual's imbalance.

Take as an example the eagerly-awaited copy of a family's

Sunday paper. There would be a free-for-all fight for the paper if it were not for the diversified interests. As it is, father takes the first section, mother the ladies' pages, the sophisticated daughter has the literary part, big brother gets hold of the sports section, the poor in spirit get the comics, the politician gets the world review.

This is not an example of *abstraction*. The paper has been *concretely* taken apart and divided among the members of the family.

Now let's have a look at the small ads. Has anybody except a proofreader ever read all the ads? McLuhan says all ads are good news; you go with hope to the position that promises fulfillment. This time, the family members leave that section intact and only abstract what is of interest. You have a choice. You can cut the advertisement out; in this case you *subtract*, the paper is less than before. Or you can *abstract*, by copying or remembering, and leave the paper intact.

If you copy the ad, this copy still belongs to the OZ; if you remember it, it enters the MZ, and if you are happy about your find, it even reaches the SZ, the zone of self.

At this point, I don't want to talk about the levels and economy of abstraction. We have as much as we need for our next step, but I want to mention that the highest degree of abstraction is the number, where every concreteness has been bracketed off, every characteristic is deleted, and only the number is left of the thing, fact, or process.

Within the number game, the impossible is made possible. For instance, a person living in South Africa can have 1.2 mosquito bites per day, while his share will go up considerably if he lives in Kenya.

Let me repeat once more our letter game. We have T for toxic and N for nourishing. We had Z for zone or locus or place where an event takes place. This placing is called topology. We have roughly distinguished OZ, the outer zone, and SZ, the self zone, the place, so to say, within the skin, and I have mentioned that *within* the SZ there is a DMZ which prevents the direct communication between self and otherness, which prevents us from being "in touch." The DMZ is often called the "mind" or consciousness, which is confusing as to what is really going on. If I feel an itch, I am conscious of it but if I say that this itch is in my mind I might be accused of being crazy.

Christian Science makes good use of this confusion. I can usually spot practitioners of Christian Science and their children by their type of confusion.

One of the two hangers-on in San Francisco was a middle-aged woman who had come to me in a schizoid state in Miami. She was reared in a Christian Science-soaked atmosphere and morality. Every signal she picked up was immediately distorted and used for her delusional system.

If we call the "mind" the *fantasy*, and use the awareness theory, we are standing on the solid ground of reality. The term *fantasy* has a key position in my Gestalt philosophy. It is as important for our social existence as the gestalt formation is for our biological existence.

It is quite common to oppose fantasy and rationality, meaning that any fantasy or imagination is a "far out" thing and rationality is called the epitome of sanity. I am using fantasy and imagination synonymously, though imagination has a somwhat more active connotation.

I want to go on vacation. So I plan. This planning is rational fantasy. I might use props from the OZ such as maps, travel agent's advice, etc., but mainly I fantasize in the form of anticipation, needs, and memory. Then I cut down or enlarge my fantasy until in fantasy or in conjunction with the travel agent I come up with a decision that fits my needs, time, and purse.

I mentioned before that all theories and hypotheses are fantasies which are of value only if they fit the observable facts.

In other words, rational fantasy is what is meant by saying, "He is of sane mind."

Reader: "All right, Fritz, I can follow you there. What about memories. You seem to include them. If you mix up fantasy and memory, you are confused or a liar."

Correct. We speak of a reliable memory, which already leaves a doubt about the general application. The thesis is that *every memory is an abstraction from an event*. It is not the event itself. If you read a newspaper, the paper itself remains in the OZ. You don't eat, swallow and digest the tangible paper itself. What is more, you select what interests you. What is more, news is reported with the bias of that newspaper's political convictions. What is more, how much of the news appears is selected by the reporter's power of observation, his opportunities, and possibly his need for sensationalism.

Reader: "I agree, but if I have an experience, I can remember it very clearly."

How much of the experience do you remember? How much are you biased? How much of the tone of voice, of hesitations, do you remember? Have you swallowed the incident, or do you recall and return to that event in reality—which is impossible, as the event is past while the returning is now. This returning gives us already much more—and much less biased—material than the frozen memories, which in fact are biased by the present position of liking or disliking.

Many investigations exist about the bias and selectivity of the memory of, say, observers of an accident. I wish you had seen the picture *Rashomon* and you could experience how differently each person interprets the same events, according to the needs of their self-esteem system.

In other words, even the most reliable observation is an abstraction. I can already see that I would have to write many more pages to make clear the key position of fantasy.

In psychopatholgy, the most important fantasies are the ones where the patient cannot realize their irrationality. The most extreme case would be a paranoid schizophrenic who imagines and truly believes that the doctor is out to kill him. To prevent this, he goes out into the OZ. That is, he actually shoots the doctor.

Many of us have catastrophic fantasies, don't bother to check them out as to their rationality, become phobic, and are not willing to take reasonable risks.

Many of us have anastrophic fantasies, don't bother to check them out as to their rationality, become reckless, and are not willing to take reasonable precautions.

Some of us have a balance of catastrophic and anastrophic fantasies; we have perspective and rational daring.

Roles and games played in fantasy are of an infinite variety, from extreme self-torture to limitless wish-fulfillment.

I wish I could stop here. Yet I have to go on to that abstraction that produced the fantasy of the existence of a "mind."

I finished up here last night and woke up with a kind of spite. "No, I won't make a big spiel. I *won't* go into the ramification of the 'word' as the abstraction of an abstraction. I *won't* go into the details of thinking as subvocal speaking, as talking in fantasy."

I will mention how much it amazes me that every time I fantasize writing about one thing, a different theme comes up, pulling some old construct out of my (this time I admit mental) garbage pail, and I learn something new. I am even willing to admit that my garbage pail does not exist at all, that I only invented it to play my reorientation game. Again, I look around. My desk is less cluttered than usual—the surf, the mountains. Do I want to write about Esalen or get dressed and go down to the lodge for breakfast?

"Getting dressed" sounds funny. I am in pajamas, and all I do is to get into one of my jumpsuits, my favored dress. I have quite a number of them. The best are the ones made of terry cloth, especially good for going to the hot baths.

I seldom walk down to the lodge. I use my little Fiat, which is 18 inches shorter than a VW. I call it my motorized baby pram. My house is perched about three hundred feet above the baths, right on the cliff. It is largely cut into the mountain, so that it has both a view over thousands of square miles of ocean and of the wild gentle cliffs stopping its relentless nagging and undermining, willing to give not more than a few boulders to the softly demanding waves.

You don't walk out of the door. You *emerge*, not, as before, into untouched nature, but into a mixture of magnificent view, natural stone steps which are an extension of the circular stone wall, and cabins and motor cars below.

Walking up and down from the lodge is no strain for most people. For me, it is. I usually drive down. From there down to the baths is a similar distance, which I have to walk. It is slowly getting easier for me to climb up. Sometimes I can do it without overstrain on my leg muscles or heart.

When I first came to Esalen, my heart was in pretty bad shape.

I want to write about my heart. I am groping for a beginning, and understanding. The garbage pail turns into a merry-go-round nightmare. The psilocybin trips, their content: near dying, near dying, giving up. No! Come back to life, come back.

The spinning ceases. I am back in the trenches. 1916. No, not in the trenches any more. I am in an army hospital. Out of the misery of the acute warfare. I had met a good man, our new doctor. We talk; he wants to know about anti-Semitism. Plenty of it, yes, even in the trenches. But mostly from the officers.

Our company is being moved to another sector of the front. I develop the flu, with high fever. He sends me to a hospital. I have a real bed. He visits me two days later. Am I fit to come along? The fever mounts and the fever *is* real, not manufactured or faked. And yet it drops once I am out of the danger zone.

The next day, I wake up with a dream: My family, in the foreground Grete, the sister I love, standing around my grave, begging me to come back to life. I strain, I pull, I make a tremendous effort, and succeed. Slowly, slowly, I am coming back to life, willing, not very willing though, to give up death, the death that was so much preferable to the horrors of war.

I had already succeeded in hardening and desensitizing myself, but there were two kinds of death I could hardly face.

One was the after-attack commandos. They climbed out of the trenches after the gas cloud had travelled over the enemy lines. They were armed with a kind of long elastic hammer, with which they clubbed and killed anyone who still showed signs of life. I never found out whether they did this to save ammunition or to avoid attention or out of pure sadistic enjoyment.

The other happened only once. We had tested our gas-masks in the morning with tear gas. They seemed to fit all right. That night, we made another gas attack. Last check of the steel bottles. The meteorologist is testing wind speed, wind steadiness, wind direction.

Hour after hour passes. Last night the attack was called off. What about tonight? Hour after hour passes. I am not very tense, sitting in my dug-out and reading some high-brow stuff. Finally the wind conditions seem to be right. Open the valves! The yellow cloud creeps towards the trenches. Then a sudden swirl. The wind changed direction. The trenches are in zig-zag lines. We might get the gas into our trenches! And we did and the masks fail with many. And many, many, get slight to severe poison and I am the only medic and I have only four small oxygen flasks and everyone is desperate for some oxygen and clinging and I have to tear the flask away to give some comfort to another soldier.

More than once was I tempted to tear my mask off my sweating face.

In 1914, when the war broke out I was already studying medicine. My medical army examination pronounced me "fit for landstorm," which is even below "fit for reserve." I stooped rather badly and had a dropheart, an elongated, small heart. I had difficulties maintaining the efforts of sports that required stamina and I preferred all types of sports of balance.

I had no intention of becoming a soldier and a bloody hero. So I volunteered to become a Red Cross soldier, to be used outside the combat zone. Much of the time I stayed in Berlin to continue my studies. After a four-week trip to Mons, on the Belgian border, I had enough and went awol, only I did not know that this was the case, as in my opinion the Red Cross was a semi-private organization. When I was caught I pretended to have a bad leg and limped rather amateurishly. I was sent to Professor Schleich, who had my admiration as one of the few, even before Groddeck, who was interested in psychosomatic medicine. He gave me a subperitoneal injection which was so painful that I was willing to accept that as a cure.

We took the trip to Mons in a very slow train that always had to wait to let front troops and ammunition pass. No food. I was so exhausted, and I fell asleep so deeply that it took me several minutes to orient myself when they woke me up. It was uncanny. I stared at them, at the walls of the coach—a complete depersonalization, an absence of any feeling or meaning.

In Mons I had station duty, to hand out coffee and other refreshments to trainloads of wounded returning from the front. When I wanted to give some water to the wounded and suffering British Tommies, the German wounded did not let me. I had my first taste and shock of the inhumanity of war.

There was one Belgian girl who fell in love with me and braved the contempt of her neighbors. She was passionate and always pleaded with me, "*N'allez pas dans la guerre, chére, n'allez pas.*" At that time I was quite good with my French and frequently served as an interpreter, especially later with the army.

In 1916 the fronts were frozen. More and more men were called up. I had a friend. I will eventually have to talk more about him. Right now I don't remember his Christian name. His family name was Knopf. We decided to volunteer for the army, before we would be called up. He chose the supply brigade and was killed through an accident. I chose the *Luftschiffer* batallion, those who worked with the Zeppelins, the dirigibles which actually played a negligible part in the war.

The sergeant of my platoon was rather fond of me. I impressed him by being a medical student. "You won't be here long anyhow. You'll be transferred to the medical corps." But I impressed him more with my shooting skill. When the captain came for inspection, he put me on the shooting stand. The truth is that in the lying position, with support, I am a good shot, but I am not fully steady in a standing position.

The ugliest thing happened with our lieutenant. To help finance the war the emperor produced the slogan: "I gave gold for iron." We were promised one day of leave for each gold coin we would bring. I collected finally four ten-mark gold pieces. When I asked for my leave I was sent to the lieutenant and received the reply: "Don't be impertinent, you swine. You should be happy to serve your Fatherland. Turn about, march!" I had several encounters of that nature with German officers. No breed in the whole world can match their monocle-clad arrogance.

I am tired and bored with war narration. I wish something exciting would come up. Some theory, some poetry, but I am sticking to my promise to write only what comes up. After all, nobody can determine the sequence in which his shit comes out.

Yet there is law and order in nature. The feces are the accumulated unused or unusable surplus from our food and they more or less come out in order of the intake. The difference between the consumed food and the feces is used by the organism for nourishment. It has been assimilated; it has become part of the self. The transition from OZ to SZ has been completed.

One of the reasons why the Freudian system cannot work is the omission of the fact of assimilation. Freud is stuck with the mentality of cannibals who fantasize that the eating of a brave warrior will give them courage.

Freud has an oral zone and an anal zone and nothing in between.

I am up early, look over this section. I don't like "it." It reads stuffy, like a school composition—oral and anal zone—stuffy, stuffy, stuffy. Why can't you just say: Freud you have a mouth and an asshole. And a big mouth; so have I. And you are an asshole and so am I. We both are pompous asses, taking us so seriously. We have to produce big theories for mankind.

I've had enough. Let's throw the whole garbage pail into a super garbage bin and have done with it.

Topdog: Fritz you can't do this. One more unfinished manuscript! Readers or not, publisher or not, you had excitements, new insights and discoveries. What if others profit by it?

Underdog: This is not the point. I am getting obsessed with words and I am becoming selective. What I see, think, and remember is being put into words viewed from a writer's point of view. This morning I felt close to insanity. Words were crawling all over me like termites.

Topdog: All the more I suggest you go on. You had times where words, feelings and thoughts came together in poetry. If you are stuck between the verbal and the non-verbal, then look at your impasse, use your theory.

Underdog: Disciplining and forcing myself is not my preaching.

Topdog: Who speaks of preaching? You yourself said over and over that any mental illness is the result of phobic behavior. You declare over and over that Freud could not finish his work, in spite of all his discoveries, because he had severe phobias. Now you are becoming phobic yourself. Now you are avoiding the pain of drudgery or a possible slight to your vanity.

Underdog: You are right and you are wrong. Sure I am phobic when it comes to insanity. I don't want to go crazy.

Topdog: Stop that nonsense immediately! You know that you are a near borderline case. You know that you had the courage to go a few times close to the border of insanity. You know that your dreams are schizy. You want to explore schizophrenia. You know how with all your pathology you managed to develop into a being of which many, many are jealous. And most of all your role on earth is not finished! You are beginning to assume a place in history, at least in psychology, perhaps in philosophy.

Underdog: Blah, blah, blah, blaaaah.

Topdog: Now Fritz, don't make me angry. And don't play the spiteful brat.

Underdog: Ha,ha,ha,ha! I got you. I can play teacher, I can play sexpot, but I must not play spiteful brat.

Topdog: Well, you are too sharp for me. So do what you want to do!

Never mind. I will. And I feel better after this conversation. I will pretend that there is no atomic bomb in the background and that I will live forever. This, at least, will take some pressure off my writing.

And I will start out with an attack on the mainstay of the piecemeal-oriented behaviorists. The famous reflex-arc, or stimulus-reaction bit, or penny-in-the-slot-machine mechanics. With the reflex-arc, the ingoing sensoric and the outgoing motoric one-way-street system, we are made into un-responsible robots ready to be manipulated by button-pushers. True, in the lower echelons we have lots of automatic-like responses and when we itch, we scratch. But the one fact alone that we can suppress the scratching shows that there is awareness involved.

As far as the conditioned reflexes are involved it has been clearly demonstrated that they disappear with time if they are not put to use.

I want to take you along for an experiment. We have three boxes: a small one *s*, a medium-sized one *m*, and a large one *l*.

Now we take s and m and an animal. We put some food every day into m. Soon the animal does not bother any more to investigate s and it makes straight for m.

Now we replace s by l, and expect the animal to go to its usual feeding place m.

But it does not. It goes for l. From this we conclude it has an orientation, and what's more it has a gestalt-directed orientation: it goes for the larger box. It goes for a constellation.

We can now not only drop the reflex-arc theory; we can replace it by a holistic organismic-concept.

Each individual has two systems with which to reach and communicate with the world. One is the senses, the sensoric system, the awareness, the means for discovery, a system that exists for the purpose of orientation.

This system dos not lead inward reflexly; the pictures or sounds of the world do not enter us automatically, but *selectively*. We don't *see*; we *look for, search, scan* for something. We don't hear all the sounds of the world, we *listen*.

If the foreground figure is very strong, if we are fascinated by the scene or some sounds, the background recedes into oblivion.

The same applies to the motoric, the muscular system, with which we approach, grasp, destroy, play, and cope with the world.

Both systems are cooperative and interdependent. In looking we move the eyeballs and the head. In listening we cock and turn the head in the direction of a sound; we might even strain to see and hear.

Reader: That sounds very plausible, but I have discovered an inconsistency in your theory. First you say everything is awareness and now you reserve awareness for the sensoric system.

No. I am not inconsistent. The senses serve the orientation towards the environment, towards the OZ. Every organism has plenty of inner senses for orientation within the organism. When we cope, we test the amount of muscle contractions, the effort required for different tasks. We pick up the signals and status of every organ, even of the bones, although the brain tissue seems to have a minimum of awareness.

Our pseudo-division—we actually deal with a cooperative—into the systems of orientation and coping gives us now a better orientation to the relationship of man to his culture. Man has expanded both systems. For improved orientation we have invented microscopes and telescopes, maps and radar, philosophy and encyclopedias, etc. For improved coping we have invented symbols and language, tools and machines, computers and conveyer belts, etc.

The reflex-arc theory misses the center. By reaching out with orientation and coping towards the world we have a center. Responsibility for our existence replaces senseless mechanics.

By far the most important extension of man's potential has been the discovery of rationality, including logic, measuring, and other number games. Also important is the use and misuse of his fantasy: inventions put to constructive and destructive use—art to enrich and debase man's relations to beauty. Religions and moral codes to free and restrict man's interaction appear to be a mixture of fantasy and rationality. The absoluteness of good and bad has to be categorically denied.

Topdog: What are you sitting there for and brooding? I know you have something up your sleeve about ethics.

Underdog: Yes, I have. But it's midnight and I am tired. I don't want to go on. I feel good about my exposition of the sensoric-motoric system.

T: Well, go to bed.

U: I am too lazy. I would like a midnight snack.

T: So, now you see what you did when you let Teddy take the refrigerator away.

U: That was at a time when its sudden noises interfered with our audio-system. We had difficulties enough with hum in the lines, the sound of the waves, the echo in the center room. I bought a lot of expensive equipment for my video adventure and we had a continuous fight with technical difficulties. Often enough I experienced man as the slave of the machine. Often enough, just when we needed the video-recorder most, it went on the blink.

T: Poor Fritz. If I have time, I'll feel sorry for you tomorrow.

U: Smart aleck. I know I didn't *have* to get involved in all this, but just imagine, if we had tapes and films of Freud, Jung and Adler. Would this not be interesting? We would not have to guess and rely on verbal descriptions alone. You know something, topdog? I begin to feel more comfortable with you. From now on I am going to call you T and myself U and we shall have many conversations together.

T: Accepted. Now what about your "readers"?

U: I might put much of their saying onto you. You are me anyhow and so probably is the reader, as he lives mostly in my imagination.

T: Good. From now on I will keep you more in line. You complained about your video-recorders. You don't seem to like gadgets.

U: On the contrary. Just dip into my garbage bin. Here are the radios I built, here are cameras and movie cameras, darkroom equipment. Here is a beaut from South Africa. A seven-foot wing-spread plane with a little motor. It actually flew. And here is a model of an invention I was very proud of.

T: It has a propeller. Is it a flying engine?

U: Not exactly. It is an every-stroke engine. It is very simple and has few moving parts. You put a two-stroke engine on each side of the propeller shaft. So you throw the piston up with one engine and down with the other and rotate the propeller along the sine curve of the sleeve.

T: That's too technical for me. Does it work?

U: The mechanical model did. I had the drawing made for the gas engine but never built the gas engine.

T: Did you take out a patent?

U: No. I never bothered. Once I could see it worked, I was satisfied.

T: You *are* stupid. You could have made a lot of money.

U: And get involved in all that red tape and negotiations and become a manufacturer and lose my freedom? No, sir!

T: Any other invention in your garbage pail?

U: Yes, a good one, but one you can't get a patent for.

T: What is it?

U: An aquafilter.

T: That's not an invention of yours. Aquafilters exist and are being manufactured.

U: Yes, but you need always a supply on hand and they are an additional bother.

T: What about the Waterford cigarette? They have a globule which you crush in the filter tip and the tip becomes an aquafilter.

U: You are coming closer. I have not seen the Waterford advertised for a long time. The one disadvantage is, you have no choice. You are restricted to that one brand.

T: Now you are making me really curious. What is your invention?

U: I invented a way to make an aquafilter from any filter tip.

T: How did you do it?

U: I blow some saliva into it.

T: I *thought* you would make a fool of me. You underdogs, whenever you are not afraid of us, you ridicule us.

U: No, no, not this time. I admit that we are good opponents. When you topdogs try to control us with bullying and threats, we control you with, "Mañana; I try so hard; I forgot; I promise." You must admit the underdog wins more often that not.

T: So what is the value of that invention?

U: I use it myself. You must not blow in too much saliva, then the cigarette paper gets soggy and you lose the tip. The water cools the hot air, the gases which carry the most poisonous stuff. Smoking becomes milder. You try it yourself.

T: Why all this fuss? Just stop smoking. You said you have a bad heart and you know how bad smoking is for that.

U: God almighty! Do we have to go into that again. Every bitch who cannot find anything else to bother me with attacks me for my smoking. No, I did not say I *have* a bad heart. I said I *had* one. I am much improved.

T: Where shall we start? With your smoking, if you think it will interest me.

U: Will you stop that sneering. We are now married for kicks and for drag till the editor us do part.

As boys we had a secret meeting place in a basement in the backyard. All we did there was smoking, depositing our shit, and declaring our independence from the grown-ups. I was eight then, and stopped smoking until the end of the war. My comrades, of course, approved of my non-smoking; they got my ration. When peace broke out—no, when the armistice came—I was in a hell of a confusion. I was glad the thing was over, although I was in a relatively comfortable position. I had become a medical sub-lieutenant and we officers ate well, at the expense of the rest of the company. My pig of a captain was an alcoholic. We had at home a good supply of Palestine wine. Each month I was sent to Berlin to fetch him a few bottles.

"This does not sound very plausible. You mean you had to travel all the way from the front just for a few bottles of wine?"

I did not *have to* but I liked to. I mostly turned it into a weeklong furlough. Being an officer, I could bring some food to my starving family, at the cost of the privates. As an officer I travelled in upholstered coaches.

When I came home for the first time after nine months in the trenches and went to bed, I got a fright. I thought I was falling through the bed. It truly was soft, compared with the little bit of straw we were used to in the rat-infested trenches.

Another time I got a ticket to a *Figaro* performance in the Royal Opera House. I was so moved by the beauty, in contrast to the dirt and suffering in the trenches, that I had to leave the theater and sobbed my heart out. This was one of the dozen or so times in my life when I was deeply shaken with emotions.

"You said you were rather comfortable during the second part of the war."

Stupid. The bed and the opera instance were long before that. They happened at my first furlough. I was still a private first-class.

After the defeat we were marching over twenty hours a day. Hardly anything to eat. It was then that I started to smoke and I have never stopped since.

Dr. Leuschke, a university professor who treated me two years later for a pleurisy attack, told me that ten not-inhaled cigarettes were equal to one deeply inhaled one. Since then I have seldom inhaled fully.

In 1963 in L.A. my heart gave me plenty of trouble. I had such agonizing anginal attacks that I contemplated suicide very seriously. Dr. Danzig, my beautiful, warm, and human cardiologist, found a bad decompensation of the heart. Drug treatment produced some improvement, but the agony persisted. And I would rather kill myself than to give up smoking.

Then I found Esalen and improved my heart tremendously. The two main factors were: I was out of the L.A. smog, and I had treatments with Ida Rolf.

Now I smoke incessantly, mainly during the sessions. I smoke mild cigarettes, sometimes even *Bravo*, that lettuce stuff, and I seldom inhale. I know that once I am rid of my self-image, I'll be able to give up that filthy habit. I know that this writing has to bring me to that point. I know that with me it is not a fear of dying, because I don't care so much about living. I know that there is still more of me hidden behind the smoke-screen. I have to be the living proof of my theory.

"You introduced a new name: Ida Rolf. How did she help you?"

With her type of physical re-conditioning. I am not ready to discuss the work of "Mrs. Elbow." Let her wait a bit longer in the garbage pail. She often kept me waiting for months, too.

"You say her work is physical re-conditioning. This sounds as if you suddenly subscribe to the mental/physical dichotomy."

No, I don't. The organism is a whole. As you can abstract the biochemical, behavioristic, experiential, etc., function and make one your specific sphere of interest, so you can approach the total organism from different aspects, provided that you realize that any change in any sphere produces a change in every other corresponding aspect.

I was quite successful in using terms like orientation which are central, unified and thus operational in many spheres. Hopefully we might one day have a language and a terminology worthy and befitting the holistic outlook. In the meantime we have to do with often clumsy circumlocutions.

One such compromise term is "psychosomatic," as if psyche and soma exist separately and come together in certain instances.

For example, in Germany, we used the term heart-neurosis for a syndrome of tachycardia, sweating, slight trembling. Some of us saw this as a result of thyroid over-activity, others as a result of a state of anxiety.

"According to your holistic outlook, it is the result of both."

No, it is not a *result*, but an *identity*.

I have plenty of justification to talk now about anxiety, especially its physiological, fantasy and coping aspects.

We call our time the age of anxiety.

Freud's definition of the neurotic's cure is freedom from anxiety and guilt.

Many psychiatrists are afraid of anxiety and avoid producing anxiety in their patients.

Goldstein sees anxiety as the result of catastrophic expectations.

As for explanations, we see again the psychoanalysts in the foreground. The past-oriented Freud comes up with the birth trauma and repression of libido, Reich and Adler with repression of agression, someone else (I forgot which of the Freudian disciples) with repression of the death-instinct. So take your choice.

I reject any explanatoriness as being a means of intellectualizing and preventing understanding.

To me the discussion of anxiety is especially important because it opens the door to the dynamic aspects of the organism's functioning.

"I don't understand your reasoning. To me, anxiety is a malfunction, a disturbing factor, reaching, as you said yourself, sometimes the status of an illness."

Patience, my dear. I admit the expression "it opens the door" is badly chosen. Will you be satisfied if I say it gives me an opportunity or excuse to—

"Yes, my dear."

Are you getting chummy? You keep quiet for a while and listen to what I have to say about "normal" dynamics, O.K.?

"O.K., but I'll be back. So mind your p's and q's. Let me just remind you of your statement that the unfinished situation provided the dynamic, that any unfinished situation will push towards completion."

Yes, how?

"By drinking water, when you are thirsty."

And where do we get the energy from? No machine or organism can function without energy.

"Well, does not the water get a libidinal cathexis?"

I admit this is a good term of Freud's for the figure/background formation. The gestaltists call it *Aufforderungs character*, character of demand. The water demands to be swallowed.

"This sounds like nonsense to me. The water would not say such a thing."

Don't be so particular. Of course the term is a poetic projection, but it is phenomenologically correct.

"So you accept the libido in this case?"

Yes, *if* you have a sexual urge for this water. Isn't it more reasonable to reserve libido for its original connotation of sexual energy?

"Then we still have to say: where does the energy to walk to the water come from."

Now you are talking and my anwer is: I don't know. I can only theorize and subscribe to an intermediate term. I can do something else in this process. I can include my theory on emotions.

I said before I don't subscribe to the defecation theory of Aristotle and Freud. I don't consider emotions a nuisance to be gotten rid of. Whether or not you consider anxiety an emotion, it will find its place in that theory.

"Then you are using the gimmick of explanatoriness?"

Partly I do, but you will see that it also will produce some real understanding about the nature of anxiety.

"All right, shoot."

If you say it so blandly, you make me unsure of how to begin. You even make me squirm somewhat.

"Now I can laugh at you. So shoot. In the beginning was what?"

In the beginning there were some terms, some general terms created by people who knew as little as I do about what the specific organismic energy is. They did not want to commit themselves to say: "It is electrical, or chemical, or libidinal, or what-not energy." So they gave it an indifferent name like Bergson's *élan vital*, or bio-energy, life energy.

I like to use the term *excitement*. Excitement can be experienced, and it has an affinity to the specific property of protoplasm, excitability. This excitement is provided by the metabolism of the organism. That one gestalt which from the survival point of view has the greatest significance gets the most excitement and is thus capable of emerging and using its excitement for orientation and coping.

In many cases this coping requires an extra-ordinary amount of excitement and this is experienced as an emotion. Excitement in this case undergoes a hormonal transformation which changes the generalized indifferent excitement into specific excitements.

We already know that anger and fear are connected with adrenalin, and sex with the procreative glands. About the hormonal situation in grief, joy, despair, etc. we know next to nothing yet.

Next step. These emotions are not just discharged, but transformed mostly into motoric energy: in anger into hitting and kicking, in grief into sobbing, in joy into dancing, in sex. . . well, I don't have to tell you about those ridiculous movements.

After the available excitement has been fully transformed and experienced, then we have good closure, satisfaction, temporary peace and nirvana. A mere "discharge" will barely bring about the feeling of exhaustion and being spent.

To sum up, excitement is both an experience and the basic form of organismic energy.

"Fritz, congratulations. This is well put. Your theory fits the facts. Maybe your transformation theory is even original. It has only one fault."

?

"You left out anxiety. Or could it be that you are mixing up fear and anxiety? In that case anxiety would be connected with adrenalin and not with thyroxin."

You are a sharp cookie. I am glad you are a part of me. But sometimes you are dumb, too. You could have realized that I, and not only I, see anxiety as an unhealthy state, while the emotions I just described are the normal emotional metabolism.

"You mean the thyroid gland is abnormal and produces anxiety?"

Don't be a dope. Listen. Stop that clowning and be serious. I am writing a serious scientific book.

"I agree that you are writing a book. Whether you are serious is another question. So what is this thyroid bit?"

I imagine that the thyroid plays the role of a general exciter, something that changes certain chemicals like carbohydrates into excitement.

"Now you are jumping from one aspect to another, from the biochemical to the psychological one."

I know. I am groping. Let's formulate it this way. The thyroid (if it is that gland) hormone turns biochemical stuff into bio-energy, like in the case of an accumulator where chemical energy is transformed into electrical power.

"I like that. Then the thyroid has nothing to do with anxiety?"

It can. Let's say for the time being that a person who produces too much thyroid—Basedow's type, a person who is overexcited—is more prone to anxiety than a normal person.

"So, what is normal?"

The zero-point of optimal thyroid production. Too little produces the cretinoid type who is underexcited, stupid and lazy. Its opposite is the Basedow-type who is go-go-go.

"Where do the chemicals come from?"

From the food we assimilate, transformed into those chemicals.

"Where does the food come from?"

From the supermarket.

"What makes you go to the supermarket?"

My hunger.

"What produces your hunger?"

The lack of those chemicals.

"Where do those chemicals come from?"

From the food we assimilate.

"Where does the food come from?"

From the supermarket. Hey! Stop that. You are playing stupid.

"No, I am playing your theory of the chicken and the egg. Well, stop wasting our time and give us something concrete!"

O.K. Can you see that anxiety is always related to the future?

"You mean Goldstein's definition that anxiety is the result of catastrophic expectations?"

You are coming closer. I go along with *expectation*. "I am anxious to see my friend." This sounds positive, not catastrophic at all.

"Yes. I can see that you are anxious to finish your book."

Now what do we *know* about the future?

"Next to nothing. Very little."

What do we know about the present?

"Quite a bit, if we let be."

Yes. I go a step further and come back to the philosophy of nothingness. The future holds plenty of possibilities, but of the actuality of this future we know *nothing*. To say the least we are not aware of anything, except through the crystal ball, if you believe in that. And even with the crystal ball we are not aware of the future, but of a *vision* of the future, just as we cannot be aware of the past, only of *memories* of the past.

Now, this is my first thesis. *Anxiety is the tension between the now and the later.* This gap is a void that usually is filled with planning, predictions, reasonable expectations, insurance policies. It is filled with habitual repetition. This inertia prevents us from having a future and hangs on to *sameness*. For most people the future is a sterile void.

Now let's go to the most frequent form of anxiety, stage fright. I am inclined to say that all anxiety is stage fright. If it is not stage fright, (that is, related to performing), then the phenomenon in question is dread. Or anxiety is an attempt to overcome the dread of nothingness often appearing in the form of nothingness = death.

When Schneider—Gelb and Goldstein's brain-injured soldier— was asked to perform an abstract task, he got deeply anxious.

"Why could he not just say that he could not or would not perform?"

Because he was *anxious* to perform. Without being *anxious to*, excited about the possibility of performing, there would be no opportunity to create anxiety.

We link up now with the second level of my neurosis theory— the role-playing level. Any time we are not sure of some of our roles, we develop anxiety.

And we link *fantasy* and Freud's dictum that thinking is re-hearsing. We rehearse for our roles, if we are not sure of them.

And we link this with the fact that all reality is the *now*, and as soon as we leave the secure position of being in touch with the present and jump into the future in fantasy, we lose the support of our orientation.

And we link self-actualization versus self-*concept* actualization, a permanent source for anxiety.

And we link the dynamic of excitement; the transformation of excitement into emotions and coping is blocked, stagnating. We get an overflow of excitement.

We understand now the role of the tranquilizer in modern psychiatry. With lobotomy we cut out the fantasy life of the patient, and with the tranquilizer we cut out his vitality, which through maldistribution of excitement has gone haywire.

Anxiety derived its connotation from the Latin word *angustia,* the narrow pass. Excitement cannot flow freely through the bottleneck that leads to the transformation. It also refers to the narrowness of the chest.

With this we have arrived at the physiological aspect of anxiety. The mobilized over-excitement needs more oxygen. So the heart begins to race to provide more oxygen, because we hold our breath in expectation.

This puts an additional strain on the heart and the doctor usually warns the cardiac patient to keep away from over-excitement.

Freud's theory of anxiety as birth trauma is a projection into the past. The breathing is out of kilter in anxiety. The repression of libido, aggression, etc. is the blocking of excitement.

I have films to show that any stage fright disappears as soon as the patient gets in touch with the present and lets go of his preoccupation with the future.

Don't push the river, it flows by itself.

I begin to realize that I am much more complicated than I expected.

I begin to realize the tremendous difficulties I will have finishing, even continuing, this writing.

I begin to realize the amount of struggle I feel between reporting and planning on the one hand and a spontaneous flow on the other.

It is getting more and more difficult to be honest and to involve living people.

Compared with that, it is easy to live in abstractions, to make up theories and play fitting games.

Does this word fit the fact? Does this gown fit the occasion? Does this accessory fit the gown? Does this theory fit the observation? Does this behavior fit the mother's wishes?

Does this shell fit the gun? This president this state? This program my potential? Fitting, fitting, fitting. Fitting and comparing. What other games are there to play? Does my living fit your expectations? Compare me with your other lovers. Am I tops?

Kaleidoscope of living. Went to the lodge. Breakfast. Nixon won on the first ballot. Anybody interested in politics?

We live in another world.

Very peculiar morning. I felt in a desperate mood—silly, unnecessary demands. Smoked a lot, lots of heartbeats missing. Wanted to withdraw, sent Teddy away. The film people who did the Fritz-Maharishi encounter were back for shooting additional footage to another scene. This was a meeting with John Farrel playing a young man in search of a solution for the American youth. We had filmed that scene in a plunge in the baths.

I was glad about that pulling me out of my whirl. Here was something simple to do.

It was a minor instance of what I had felt when I volunteered for the army. Unexpectedly the training was a great relief from responsibility. I was told how to greet an officer, how to march, make a bed, etc. No choices, no decisions.

Like in the high school days, I went back to living several lives at once.

My days in the *Mommsen gymnasium* had come to an end. That school was a nightmare for me. In the elementary school I took it for granted that I was top of my class. I liked my teacher and school was child's play. As a matter of fact, I could already read and I knew the multiplication tables before I entered school.

I notice how quickly I am regressing from filming to army to high school to elementary school to preschool days.

Do I want to start from the beginning?

Actually we have it all wrong, when we say look forward to the future. The future is a void and we walk, so to say, blindly with our *backs* towards it. At best we see what we left behind. Now I look into a distant past. Most of it is in a fog; some abstractions seem to be correct. They are, as the dianetic people would say, in my memory filing cabinet. Some are exact replicas without a shadow of a doubt. A father, a mother, two elder sisters, familiar relatives from mother's side and some strange ones from father's. The house we moved into when I was about four years old—and where we lived for about twelve years.

When I visited Berlin for the first time after World War II I saw with a symbol-like amazement that the whole block was razed to the ground with the exception of that one house: *Ansbacher Strasse 53*.

My earliest memory is my conception.

"Now, this is tops. I know that you have a good fantasy at times, but this is so crazy that you cannot possibly put this over."

I said my *memory*. I cannot possibly say that it happened that way. I am not given to facile interpretations and if you want to accept this as a symptom of my madness, you are welcome.

I have taken much LSD, and psilocybin only a dozen times or so. To me psilocybin is mainly a recall and integrative drug. The first three sessions started with a confluence of two opposing energies. They diminished in intensity and were not present after the third. One force was intensely colorful and was experienced as invading *me*. In very slow rhythm, waves of about one minute duration, this force permeated a very reluctant and foglike me.

"How do you make a conception out of that? You did not experience yourself as a sperm and an ovum."

That is correct. You could call it the Yin and Yang or male and female substance in the sense of Weininger. He says, and I believe he is right, that each one of us has male and female substance and that the pure male man and the pure female woman are rare. My own observations tend to confirm this. In many neuroses, and many psychoses as well, I saw the male and female substances in severe conflict; in the genius I see the opposites integrated. The right/left split is pronounced in neurosis, and ambidexterity is pronounced in the genius.

"And then they are in balance?"

I see a perfect balance in Leonardo da Vinci. Michelangelo has a greater amount of maleness and Rainer Maria Rilke, greater femaleness.

"And where do you come in?"

It took me a long time to accept it when people called me a genius. It took me another three months not to care one way or another.

However, I believe strongly in integration. I have unified quite a few of my opposing forces and there is still more to come. By now, I believe, it has become clear that Gestalt Therapy is not an analytical but an integrative approach. This will become even clearer when we are ready to discuss therapy.

"Do you remember your birth?"

No. I have taken a number of patients through a kind of birth experience. In one of my tape-films "Louise," you can witness such a case. We worked on a dream and a scream which were clear indications of an incomplete birth. One of the interesting facts was the development of her screaming from the sounds of a newly born to an angry, hungry child. It is interesting that there was no anxiety whatsoever involved. This film will be part of a multi-media book: *Eyewitness to Therapy.*

My own birth recall is limited to a session with carbon dioxide when I woke up in a position and movements of the just born. And I still have a yawn like a hippopotamus or an early infant. I have been told that I was a forceps birth, that I was not properly nursed on account of a nipple infection of my mother's and that I had subsequently a near fatal *Brechdurchfall*, vomiting and diarrhea. I never had a recall of any of that.

"Would you say you had a happy childhood?"

Definitely, up to the time of the *gymnasium*. I liked school and ice-skating. I was close to my sister Grete. She was a tomboy, a wildcat with stubborn curly hair. The man she married, name of Soma Gutfreund, was a kind of nobody, a violin repairer, dealer and player. His playing could not have been too bad, as Piatigorski came to their shop to play quartets. I could not take to him. He had the ability to produce platitudes as if they were pearls of wisdom. They too, like so many other Jews, did not leave Germany until the SS entered their shop and smashed most of the instruments.

By that time havens for Jewish refugees were already scarce, but they succeeded in getting to Shanghai, where they suffered from heat and some war, from there to Israel where they suffered from food shortage, until I got them into the States, where he, at least, suffered from language trouble.

He died a few years ago, but Grete has adjusted herself. She is very nervous, very talkative and very worried. In spite of this we love each other and she takes great pride in the fact that her black sheep of a brother is becoming famous. "If only Mama could have experienced it." She is always sending me the most expensive and delicious European candies.

Mama would indeed have been very proud. She was very ambitious for me and not at all the "Jewish mother" type. But then my father kept her short of money and we were glad if we had enough to eat. She was a good cook, but never forced us to eat. Her father was a tailor and considering her background, her interest in art—especially in the theater—was amazing. She saved pennies so that we could have standing places at the Kroll Theater, an annex to the Imperial Opera and Theater. She also wanted me to have violin and swimming lessons. He gave us no money for either. She could not afford the violin, only the swimming lessons. I became a real water rat.

I disliked Else, my eldest sister. She was a clinger and I always felt uncomfortable in her presence. She also had severe eye trouble. I thoroughly disliked the idea that one day I would have to look after her, maybe burdened with her presence in my house, a heavy chain for a gypsy.

When I heard of her death in a concentration camp, I did not mourn much.

"And you did not feel guilty?"

No, I felt always resentful towards her.

"What has one to do with the other?"

Behind every feeling of guilt is resentment.

"How does resentment change into guilt?"

You have to take my word for it. I would have to go into the whole topology for that.

"Come on, do it."

No, I won't.

"Guilt and resentment are emotions. How do you get rid of them? Beating your breast with: *Pater pecavi?*"

No, this does not help.

"But you have to get rid of it to be healthy. Didn't Freud say an individual is healthy if he is free from anxiety and guilt? You are doing therapy. So, explain!"

Nag, nag, nag.

"You can't do this to me. You're forgetting we are one and we are playing a game. You procrastinate and I *resent* that."

And you don't feel *guilty?*

"No, but *you* should."

It feels much nobler to feel guilty than resentful, and it takes more courage to express resentment than guilt. With expressing guilt you expect to pacify your opponent; with expressing resentment you might stir up hostility in him.

Reading over this paragraph I get a distinct impression of playing a role again, the role of the professor. I don't mind playing roles. I don't like this dryness, lack of involvement. I like myself much better when I think or write with passion, when I am turned on.

"Let excitement reach the pen
Bellow like a thunder
Never mind if now and then
You produce a blunder.

"Rather be alive and fail
All your dear ambition
Throw right in the garbage pail
All that lacks nutrition.

"Let me dance and give me joy
Good or lousy weather.
Don't be anxious, don't be coy,
Let us dance together!

"I resent it if you bore.
This I can't admire:
Fucking like a frigid whore
'Stead of burning fire.

"*I* resent it if you don't
Give me all and neatly.
I demand that you invest
What you are, completely.

"I demand that you are here
In the now and direct!
Passionate and crystal clear!
I want you just perfect!!!"

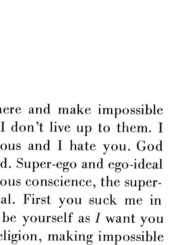

You son of a bitch! You just sit there and make impossible demands. You want me to feel guilty if I don't live up to them. I more than resent you for that, I am furious and I hate you. God almighty. You are mixing me up like Freud. Super-ego and ego-ideal being identical! No, sir! You are the righteous conscience, the super-ego, and you want *me* to be the ego-ideal. First you suck me in with: "Just be yourself," and then: "Just be yourself as *I* want you to be." You use the gimmick of every religion, making impossible demands and then extracting your pound of flesh "as if" I am in debt, "as if" I owe you something.

I am now a guide to a group of travellers:

Ladies and gentlemen, we are now leaving the country of the organism and its neat recovery of imbalances. We let the organism complete its own unfinished situations.

We are now entering the country of social behavior with its imbalance and its unfinished situations. This is the country of "shouldism," of demands. The country of imperatives.

"You think you are funny?"

No, not really. I tried to be. Sometimes I can be very funny, a really good entertainer. I cannot do it deliberately. It has to be in context.

I wanted to create a transition for the discussion on "interpersonal relations" as Sullivan called his approach, but it turned out to be a phony gimmick.

"If you are stuck, I suggest you go back and do some mopping up."

For example?

"You left so much incomplete."

Nothing exciting is coming up. No unfinished situation emerges.

"What about Ida Rolf? I'd like to know how she helped you. Or could you talk about the organismic function of resentment and guilt?"

No, I could not in regard to guilt. Guilt is a social phenomenon and resentment an organismic one. The mixing up of organismic and social functions is one of the weaknesses in the Freudian theory.

The oral and the genital stages are organismic. The anal stage is social. It is a product of premature training in cleanliness. Thus Freud's organismic theory is incorrect. The libido, his inflated term for excitement, does not jump from the mouth to the anus to the genitals. The observations about infantile sexuality and anal difficulties, including Abraham's thesis of the anal character, however, are invaluable.

"I see you yawning. You don't seem excited about this discussion. Can't you let go of Freud? He did his thing and you are doing yours."

Don't you see? I do this to clarify my own outlook. Furthermore, most of the psychiatrists believe in Freud. When Darwin developed his evolution theory he could not avoid getting involved with the believers in the Bible.

I interrupted here and went to the typewriter to continue my training that I have taken up again a few days ago. For the first time I typed a sentence relating to this book.

I am yawning, yawning. I am avoiding going into my anal difficulties and the fight with my mother about my constipation. I only know that she gave me suppositories made from soap and I hated her for that. The rest is conjecture.

I am yawning, yawning, yawning. It's still early, not even eleven o'clock. Often I write until two o'clock or even later.

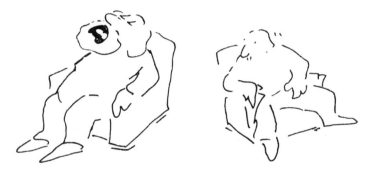

Topdog, you are right. We have some mopping-up operations to do. The pieces that come up—Freud, Ida Rolf, constipation, loss of excitement, a premature going into social relations—don't form a gestalt yet.

Teddy said that the previous writing went zigzag, in schizy-like associations.

"She is right. Let's find out where we are."

As soon as you say that I start groping, searching, yawning, sluggish, though I slept nine hours. I've got to wait until something comes up, or in shit language, until something comes out.

Yawning, yawning. This begins to become a symptom. Boredom? I started this book as an antidote to boredom. I got excited, released much energy. I am getting excited with the idea: Does this new wave of boredom herald another source of energy? Is this state of boredom an implosive state?

"That could be. It fits into the mopping-up theme. You have not spoken about implosion. Remember your neurosis theory?"

And how! The impasse. The Russian *sick point*? The center of the neurosis? Yes, it's high time to talk about it. And to bracket off ruminations and keep them at bay. Implosion. A good word. Explosion: Unrestricted power centrifugally flying into space. Emotional explosion: engulfing the world with fury and love. Frightening power, harness it! Deviate it, sublimate it! Can't always be done. All or nothing. Explode it or implode it!

Implosion, the power of contracting, the power of gravity. Without that power the earth would fall to pieces, would float, disintegrate. Implosion, a new word to the average man's vocabulary. It is here to stay. I read recently that the submarine *Scorpion* has imploded—12,000 feet of water pressure. The hull could not resist any longer, caved in. The ship, diminished in size, lies with its crew compactly on the ocean's floor. Our emotional implosions are not that strong, as our emotional explosions are not of such magnitude.

In a diesel engine the piston compresses, implodes the gas, generating sufficient heat for explosion, for a *harnessed* explosion. In other motors we have to spark that explosion. In our cells we have probably millions of mini-explosions, immeasurably small quantities of harnessed explosion. The sum of those mini-explosions are the life force, excitement.

The day when we will be able to harness the atomic explosion might be the day of world peace. There will be available more than enough energy for any country in the world. Wars for the control of energy resources will be obsolete.

In the meantime we have to understand more about the rhythm of explosion and implosion.

In the meantime we have to learn to distinguish between true implosions and pseudo-implosions.

True implosions are *no-thing*ness.

Pseudo-implosions are *nothing*ness.

True implosions are petrifaction, death.

Pseudo-implosions are potential violence, like a scale that has come to an uneasy rest. Like that trench warfare in 1916 with millions locked into each other in stalemate, like a tug of war with opposing forces, exactly matched, like the deeply withdrawn catatonic who might explode into incredible violence.

Cope and withdraw, contract and expand, implode and explode—like the heart imploding, contracting, and then exploding, opening to be filled. Permanent contracting leads to quick death, as does permanent extension.

Pseudo-implosion in the neurotic is paralysis, pseudo-death. It is filled with the excitement of two antagonists cancelling each other out.

Pseudo-implosion is *hallucinated* as death.

Pseudo-implosion manifests itself as the hollow man, the deadly bore, the bureaucrat.

Pseudo-implosion shows up in dreams as desert, buildings, and things. No vegetation, no people.

Pseudo-implosion is seen by Freud as death instinct with but one possible explosion: aggression.

Pseudo-implosion is seen by Reich and Lowen as an armor, to be opened for temporary emotional explosions or discharges.

Pseudo-implosion gets a respite by Schutz and other "turner-onners." Inhibitions thrown into the violent winds.

"You seem to find faults with everybody."

If anyone had hit the bull's-eye we would have found "the" cure by now. In any case, the Reichs and Schutzes are much closer to reality than the "mind-fuckers."

"?"

Those intellectuals, the verbiage producers.

Have you ever been to what passes for group therapy? Everybody throws his opinion on a victim, everybody interprets everybody. Argumentations, verbal ping-pong games, at best an attack: "You are projecting, my dear" or a "poor me" cry-baby performance. What kind of growth can you expect in these "self-improvement clubs"?

"You really are hard on those people. They try and mean well."

I know. It is so uncompromisingly hard to bring home that insights and discharges of emotions are not enough; that the so-called cure is part of a maturation process; that the aim of a cure is, to use Selig's expression, to teach people to wipe their own asses. In this respect, some of the "self-expresssion" teachers—especially if they are engaged in mass production—might even be harmful if they don't start from *where* the patient is, but instead give him orders about what he *should* experience. To please the teacher, the workshop participant will produce a counterfeit of that experience and only reinforce his neurosis.

"Can you give an example?"

Yes. I have seen a teacher, whether the participant felt it or not, force him to produce anger by hitting a mattress and shouting "No. No." This verbal "No" and his complying action that says "Yes" to the teacher are contradictory and can only produce confusion. This is fine if the "No" is just below the threshold of self-expression, if the *self* is involved and the whole thing is not just a gimmick of an insensitive teacher. Many therapists act out their control-madness on improvement-seeking believers, instead of over-coming that symptom in themselves.

"You are pretty mad and you are preaching now! What about yourself?"

This is one sphere where I cannot find fault with myself. I would not be where I am without my sensitivity, timing and intuition. Even when I carry out group experiments, they are so constructed as to take into account the place where each one is at that moment.

"Give me an example."

I would ask each member of a group to say a sentence starting with: "I resent—" and then follow up with finding out whether this is an empty verbal statement produced to please me, or a real experience. In that case I take the next step. "Make your demands explicit." Or have a fantasy encounter with that person until the resentment is resolved.

"How do you resolve a resentment?"

A resentment is a kind of hanging-on bite. If you resent, you are stuck with it. Often you have a mouth implosion, a tight rigid jaw. You can neither let go—forget and forgive, nor bite through—become aggressive and attack the real or imagined frustrator. Resentment, like vindictiveness, is a good example of an unfinished situation.

"Then a loosening up of the jaw is not the complete job?"

Then the loosening up of the jaw is as one-sided as "talking about" the resentment.

"Thank you, Fritz, for the lecture. I've got a good notion about implosion, I learned something more about resentments, and most of all I begin to realize some complications in doing therapy. I agree that any partial approach like bursting the armor or talking about experiences is one-sided and thus inefficient."

Yes. And I especially condemn those one-siders if they believe that their segmental approach is a panacea, a cure-all.

"Would you say that this one-sided approach also applies to Ida Rolf's "physical" re-conditioning? What is she doing? Is she doing something like the armor-busting of the Reichians?"

Sometimes she does. I would rather call this an accidental by-product, especially if you have a muscular abstraction as a memory.

"I don't understand this at all. This really sounds like gobble de gook to me: a muscular abstraction of a memory!"

I spoke about conditioned rats whose brains were pulverized and fed to others. That substance had a real memory or *mneme*, organismic memory.

Now, any incident has several aspects: the words that are spoken, the emotions we feel, the pictures we see, movements we observe, thoughts and associations we have, a pain we sense, etc. From all those thousand impressions we abstract a certain number to be filed away in our memory bank to serve as the official representative of that incident. They usually become a kind of stereotyped cliché. We might even adorn it or delete some of it.

Now if one abstraction comes up, then often the total context becomes available. This is not a linear association, although it is often called so, but a comprehensive gestalt.

Thus, if Ida touches a sore spot, which is what the muscles remember, then the total context, including the unexpressed emotions and pictures, might come up and be made availalbe for assimilation and integration.

By itself this recovered memory has as little value as the recovered memories of Freud or Reich. But if a patient hangs on to a postural fault—"as if" he is still in the original pain—then he has got the same chance of re-adjusting to the correct posture as the patient who hangs on to a dead mother—"as if" he still has to please her; he can realize that he has to please her no more, that he has been a victim of a hallucination. Both cases are "waking up" processes.

"And Ida really helped you with your heart trouble?"

This I cannot say. She certainly helped me with the main symptom: those angina pectoris pains that made life so miserable that I was willing to end it all. In this sense she saved my life.

"Did she break through to some memories?"

No. That I did with a psilocybin trip. No, her work was quite different. Those breakthroughs are merely a by-product, not an essential. Similarly to me, she works on a person's imbalance. The Reichians have an *heuristic* approach. They break the armor where they expect to find repressions. Ida has a *holistic* outlook, she looks at the whole body and tries to relocate whatever is out of kilter. She tears the sheath around the muscles apart to give the muscles breathing space, as she says, and she stimulates atrophied muscles.

"This tearing apart must be pretty painful."

Sometimes agonizing. I usually have a cigarette break after twenty minutes.

"Why does she not do this under an anesthetic?"

She claims she needs cooperation. In some places the muscle tissue is imploded and she works until you let go of the spasm.

I've had about fifty treatments. Usually she gives a planned series of ten.

"Are you through now?"

Not at all. First consider my age and that many of my implosions are very deep-seated. Only a small percentage of the improvement is retained. She has some good pupils now. One day I will be a naughty boy and try to be "Rolfed" under nitrous-oxide, laughing gas.

"So what is the connection with your heart trouble?"

In angina pectoris the muscles around your heart and in the left arm become very painful. This is probably nature's way of stopping you from overworking your sick heart. So Ida opened up the cramps in all those muscles and I could breathe freely. I also had sometimes very painful, paralyzing backaches which have improved about 80-90%. Altogether you see that I have all the reasons to be deeply grateful.

"What kind of a person is she?"

A very powerful big angel. We are now combining Gestalt Therapy with her methods. Since I brought her to California, the interest in her work grows.

"How old is she?"

She must be my age.

"If she is that good, why is she not famous?"

It is the old story of advertising something good as a panacea. She is, of course, biased and is persuasive rather than factual, sometimes taking credit for something that is not the direct result of her work. Now in co-ordination with our work something good is emerging. People with deep mental kinks will not benefit fully from her, and people with chronic postural disturbances will limit the effectiveness of our therapy. We will even investigate if our co-operation will work with schizophrenics.

Structure and function are identical: Change a structure and you change its function; change a function and you change its structure.

"You said that you recovered some memories under psilocybin. Did you remember how you got your heart trouble?"

No, not exactly. This is a much more complicated story and it centers around Marty. I wish I could simply say that Marty broke my heart, but that would be a great oversimplification. The fact is that I went through a period of suffering equal to the time in the trenches. The difference is that in the trenches I could experience myself as a victim of circumstances; with Marty I carry the responsibility.

What brought me to Miami Beach, where Marty lived, I could not exactly say. When we lived in South Africa I loved to vacation in Durban. We usually stayed at the Balmoral Hotel. A frontroom to the ocean cost a guinea, which at that time was about four dollars. That included good food with dozens of delicious salads. A broad white sandy beach and, oh boy, that Indian Ocean! Warm waves to be dived under. Plenty of time to read. Drives into Zululand, the valley of the 1000 hills. Drives with the *Zuluriksha*, the powerful Negro in warrior dress jumping into the air, tilting the riksha like a horse that is enjoying himself.

I found nothing of that sort, of course, in plastic Miami Beach, but swimming, the only sport left to me, pulled me there from New York.

I never liked New York with its hot humidity during summer and slush in winter, with its parking difficulties and sirens, with its usually atrocious theater performances and long-distance travelling in noisy, overcrowded subways. Most of all I felt more and more uncomfortable with Lore, who always put me to a disadvantage, and who at that time never had a good word to say about me.

This in turn increased my tendency to have love affairs without any deep emotional involvement. That involvement finally happened in Miami with Marty.

Big Sur, California

Dear Marty,

When I met you, you were beautiful beyond description. A straight strong Greek nose, which you later destroyed to get a "pretty" face. When you did this, when you had your nose baptized, you became a stranger. You had everything in excess—intelligence and vanity, frigidity and passion, cruelty and efficiency, recklessness and depression, promiscuity and loyalty, contempt and enthusiasm.

When I say you *were*, I am not correct. You still *are*, and you are very much alive, though more consolidated. I still love you and you love me, no longer with passion, but with trust and appreciation.

When I look back on our years, what comes up first is not our fierce lovemaking and our even more fierce fights, but your gratefulness: "You gave me back my children."

I found you despondent, nearly suicidal, disappointed in your marriage, chained down by two children, with whom you had lost touch.

I was proud to take you up and to mold you to my and your needs. You loved and admired me as therapist and, at the same time, became my therapist, cutting with your cruel honesty through my phoniness, bullshit and manipulations. Never was so much equal give and take between us as then.

Then came the time when I took you to Europe. Paris, some insane jealousy bouts on my part, some wild orgies, exciting, but not really happy. That happiness came in Italy. I was so proud to show you real beauty, as if I owned it and to help you overcome your mediocre taste in art. Of course we got drunk with Venice and. . .

That Aida performance in Verona! An ancient Roman amphitheater holding twenty—thirty thousand people. The stage? No stage. The one end of the theater built up in giant three-dimensional life-like props, a slice of Egypt transported from another continent. It is night, nearly dark. Sections of the audience lit with hundreds of candles. Then the performance. Voices floating with gripping intensity over us and through us. The finale: torches flaming into infinite space and dying voices touching eternity.

It was not easy to wake up to the hustle and bustle of the leaving crowd.

The open air opera in Rome was an artifact by comparison, never letting you forget that you are attending a performance.

Our nights. No pressure to go home, no fear of getting too little sleep. Getting the last drop from our experiencing each other. "Tonight was the best" became a stock phrase, but it was true, an ever-increasing intensity of being there for each other. There is no poetry to describe those weeks, only amateurish stutter.

In this life you don't get something for nothing. I had to pay dearly for my happiness. Back in Miami I became more and more possessive. My jealousy reached truly psychotic proportions. Whenever we were separated—and we were most of the day—I got restless, checked up on you, drove several times a day by your house. I could not concentrate on anything except: "Marty, where are you now, with whom are you now?"

Until Peter came into our life and you fell in love with him. He did not care much about you. For you, he was a respite from me and my torturing. He was easy-going, an entertaining *raconteur*. It was impossible to be bored in his presence. He was young and beautiful and I was old and vicious. To complicate matters still further: I, too, was, and still am, fond of him.

The heavens caved in for me. I was left with debasing myself on the outside and nursing wild revenge fantasies on the inside.

All attempts to break off with you failed. Then I did something which, looking backwards, appears an attempt to commit suicide without the stigma of such a cowardice.

I survived those operations. I survived our separation. I survived our final fights and reconciliation. I am here and you are there. It feels good and solid whenever we meet again.

Thank you for being the most important person in my life.

Looking back on my life I see several suicidal periods. In German the word is *Selbst-morder*, killer of himself; and this is exactly what a suicidal person is. He is a killer; he is a killer who destroys himself rather than another.

Both the killer and the suicidal have something else in common. An *impotence* to cope with a situation and they choose the most primitive way: explosion into violence.

And a third factor: I beat you to the punch. I will kill myself before you kill me.

And often: I pay my debt.

And also the opposite: I make you feel guilty: "Look what you have done to me."

And moralism rears its ugly head: punishment.

I punish myself, I punish you. The church will punish me. A suicide does not deserve to lie among the respectable dead.

And behind it all: the suicidal's redeeming fantasy: "Which miracle worker will save me?" "Will the *deus ex machina* arrive in time?"

For a psychiatrist I have, through luck and understanding, a rare record: 30 years without a single suicide among my patients.

Thirty years ago, in 1938, I treated a young Jewish man for his homosexuality. As with so many homosexuals, he had a bitchy witch of a mother. One day he came with the news that his mother had been killed, probably by the Negro houseboy. Soon after—it was *Yom Kippur*, the Jewish day of atonement—he killed himself.

Did he kill his mother? Did he have such a confluence with her that he wanted reunion in heaven? What role did atonement play?

Idle speculations! I begin to understand something new. For days I have sudden spells of tiredness, letting go of my senses, of the OZ. Withdraw. Not completely. Don't fall asleep. Don't go all the way down into oblivion.

The fertile void is boiling. The sterile void, the world of boredom is gone. How to harness the richness of the fertile void? This is more than a garbage pail, more than just obsolete stuff coming up.

But it is too much: thoughts, emotions, pictures, judgments. Too much excitement. Gestalt formation is in danger; schizophrenic-fractionalism, chaotically manifesting its right to be, overwhelms me.

Stay in touch, take your tiredness to dampen the hysteria of too many voices screaming for attention. Simmer down. Stay with Heisenberg's principle: observed facts change through being observed!

Tiredness, I took you, like boredom, for my enemy. I took you for something that wants to deprive me of a part of my life. You know how greedy I am. More and more and more.

Fertile void, speak *through* me
Let me be in grace
Let a blessed true me
See you face to face.

Write a thousand pages
Hundred thousand words
Stop to be a-cagey
That is for the birds!

As the pen is sliding
Bleeding joy and pain
I can't more abiding
Than I lived in vain.

Finally I know that
I have much to say!
What I have discovered
Is now here to stay.

Rum tura ta*ti*ta
Let us dance and jump
Ratatita*tu*ta
No more throaty lump.

Not bemoaning what I am,
I am wata*ku*ka
Uhsa pusa roma tom
Vas is da to looka?

Yippee!!! I am crazy!!!

"Now you have declared yourself insane. Where does it leave you? You want to shed all responsibility?"

Gosh, are you stuffy! This was an outburst of joy. And something else. I can't carry a tune very well. I heard music and sounds were there and I did not feel the need to fill the sounds with words. I know there is music in the fertile void.

I have a peculiar relation to singing, as if I am afraid I will disappear when I am in confluence with another voice or sound. I sometimes carry the bass well, and once, when Alma Neumann, a friend of my college days, played a Bach cantata, I sang the whole cantata correctly just by sight and ear. This miracle happened only once, but it indicates that somewhere, hidden and blocked, a great musical potential is waiting.

"Come on, don't fool me. You want to get away from the serious question of your insanity."

Oh no, not at all. I only want you to understand that this "feeling crazy" has little to do with insanity. If you call my jealousy outbursts psychotic, I go along with you. They were compulsive. I had them with Lore, I had them with Marty, and to a much lesser degree on other occasions. I understand them very well and I can explain them, which only shows how little value insights are.

Usually there were four factors involved—projections, an insatiable sexual curiosity, fear of being left out, and homosexuality.

I suddenly realized that I left out one person, Lucy, who also was an important woman in my life.

I also see how difficult it is to be a writer, even if one restricts one's self to mere facts. I have to make a choice. But, what the hell. I don't have to produce a good book. I know anyhow that my primary motive was and is to sort myself out and to do my own therapy. There is really nobody else. There was Paul and there was Marty and there is Jim Simkin and somehow I am not ready to surrender to him. Lore is not a good therapist for me. We are too competitive. She is opinionated, righteous, and does not listen. I have no doubt that she is often right, but she is, at least with me, always aggressively right.

The book thing is an additional bonus. I am keen to have people read this manuscript in my presence, to experience their participation. I need much affirmation. If I would exclusively write for myself I would leave out much of the theoretical stuff and I want to get that across.

Apparently, as I see it more and more, it is my greed again. I am greedy both ways: to have more and more experiences, knowledge and success, and to give all I have—and even this seems to be never enough.

Nowhere is the greed more expressed than in smoking. One coffin nail after the other. Bum, bum, bum. You die from smoking, you die from masturbation. I've seen many deaths from war, from illness, from accidents. I have not seen deaths from smoking and sex.

"This is not the point, as Lore would say."

So what is the point?

"You know very well, as Lore would say, hiding her ignorance behind an all-knowing face."

I don't want to talk about Lore yet, though Lucy points in that direction. "If" I had not been in trouble with Lucy I would not have gone to Frankfurt and I would not have met Lore. "If" I pull Lucy out of her coffin, I also have to pull Uncle Staub out of his most honorable coffin.

Uncle Staub was the pride of the family. He was Germany's greatest legal theoretician. He had a long beard and walked with dignity. His wife and children were stuck up and had very little to do with us. They also lived in the *Ansbacher Strasse*, while Grete and I lived on the street itself. Sister Else clung to mama.

Can you imagine? There were no motor cars yet. The street belonged to us children, except to those of the nobler classes, like the Staub children, who were too busy being educated by governesses.

Uncle Staub crossed my life as a symbol, as an interpretation and as a psychological discovery.

The symbol status was obvious, and it was obvious that I should follow his steps. But I rebelled and sneaked my way into the humanities through the sick path of medicine.

The interpretation was provided by Wilhelm Reich. He never revealed to me how he came to that conclusion: He said that I was Herman Staub's son, which appealed to my vanity and never reached conviction.

The psychological discovery came through Lucy. She told me that he had screwed her when she was thirteen. When she told me that, I had not yet examined her credibility gap and believed her. I got a confirmation of a similar thing later from another source.

Right now I feel a confusion similar to then.

I had observed quite a bit of leching in my father, but then my father was supposed to be bad in any case. And here was Germany's leading legal authority committing the crime of seducing a minor. And all that facade of respectability! And there were the teachings of Freud, apparently saying yes to sex.

"You are suddenly becoming a moralist."

I've had my spells of moral indignation. I had the first at the age of four. I was playing in the street. A little girl ran out of the house to a tree and pee'd in front of me. It's incredible! Why can't she do it at home on her potty?

"If you would write your case history as a sex-pervert, where would you put yourself with Lucy?"

I would say that this was the turning point. Up to then I had a somewhat promiscuous love-life, but basically healthy.

"Then you blame Lucy?"

No, I certainly don't *blame* her. I gladly went along with her teaching and her recklessness of exploring. And the image of the secret life of Herman Staub added a license, nearly a demand, for following his footsteps—if not in law, at least in his anti-law doings, whether they were real or Lucy's imagination.

"Was she a relative of yours, too?"

A distant relative.

"How did you meet her?"

In a very peculiar way. "They" had moved into an apartment next to ours in a "better" neighborhood than *Ansbacher Strasse*.

Lucy's and my mother knew each other. I had already put out my shingle. Lucy was in a hospital for the removal of a kidney. Her mother asked me to visit her daughter.

There I saw a beautiful blonde. One of those I liked to put on pedestals and venerate as goddesses. After ten minutes of conversation she said: "You are beautiful, come kiss me!" That floored me: What! This could happen to me? With rare exceptions, I saw myself as ugly, and here was a goddess coming from Olympus to bless a mortal? And a woman with children and husband?

My initial awkwardness melted quickly under her passionate, operation-forgetting kisses. I was gladly hooked.

I have loved a few times. The first was Katy, the blonde baker's daughter. I was eight then. Later I loved Lotte Cielinsky and more than with anybody else I was in love with Marty. With Lore I had some on-and-off periods of love, but basically we are co-travellers who have a number of interests in common.

Lucy fascinated and excited me. She was very possessive and loved me as much as she was capable. For me she was just a glorious adventure.

"You are gossiping. You are talking *about* her. Talk *to* her."

I can't talk to you, Lucy. You are dead. Dead. When I tore myself away in 1926, you ceased to exist for me. Your real death did not mean much to me. I heard that you had become a morphine addict and finally killed yourself.

"What made you go to Frankfurt?"

One of my mother's brothers lived there, Uncle Julius, an unpretentious warm person to whom I felt close as a child. *And* Karen Horney, my Berlin analyst advised me to leave Berlin *and* to continue my analysis with Clara Happel, one of her pupils. *And* Goldstein's work attracted me *and* existential groups *and* Frankfurt itself which at that time was a beautiful and cultured city.

"Is there anything else you want to say to Lucy?"

You know, topdog, I don't like you at all today. You are stuffy, matter-of-fact, nearly like a professional therapist or a Sunday-school teacher. You are not being helpful at all to bring back those sick, exciting times with Lucy.

"Shut up. What picture comes up first?"

A slit in the sliding door between my consulting room and the physiotherapy room. Lucy and a girl-friend making love in the consulting room. I am peeking through the door getting more and more excited, anxiety loaded to the bursting point. When the friend begins to suck Lucy's genitals I explode, jump into the room, push the girl aside and have a short and strong orgasm with Lucy.

The girls then arrange a quartet with the friend's husband and me. I am looking forward to my first homosexual adventure. Before that I had, in my puberty years, a minor thing with a boy, a never-touch-each-other parallel masturbation with Ferdinand Knopf. I've remembered his Christian name lately, and some loving tender feelings toward my medic when I was a medical sub-lieutenant.

Actually the husband and I were strangers and bored with each other and never got any excitement, much less any erection; but we both enjoyed watching the performance of the girls.

"How do you feel about revealing all this in public?"

I feel as if this is the hardest task I have ever undertaken. "If" I have the guts to go through with all this I will possibly be through the great impasse. "If" I can brave the real or imagined contempt and moral indignation, I'll become still more real—freer to face people and possibly give up my smoke screen. I know that I am in this respect like Wilhelm Reich, brazen, suppressing much embarrassment.

Yesterday I gave a session on dreamwork to Jim's class. As usual, it went well. I worked with five or six people and each time I succeeded within 10-20 minutes to get to the essence of each person, even to re-integrate some disowned material. This has become routine, child's play. I am never satisfied.

One of them was a blind therapist. I asked her when she became blind. She said at birth, lack of vitamins. Her dream contained pictures and she said that she felt *red* in the face, whereupon I expressed my suspicion of her blindness. How can she have pictures, how does she know what red is? I know that with my suspicion I put a seed in her. It will grow and if I am right, she will one day see again. Who knows?

Something else happened that is remarkable. During a group session, about two weeks ago, a white kitten came along with the group. A similar white kitten appeared today. It resembles Mitzie, except that its fur is less furry, but a light gray streak on the forehead is the same. She stayed after the group left. I gave her a fig bar, the only eatable thing in the house, and she ate it with gusto. Will she stay?

She follows me into my bedroom, walks curiously and yet familiarly all over the place. She does not want to walk out through the opened deck-door, settles comfortably on the bed, snuggles into my hand. Shall I keep her, again be bothered with care and maintenance? I don't know yet. I'll set her out into the hall. She can sleep in the center room if she insists on staying.

"I see you made a drawing of your house. Are you again running away from the theme? What about your sex life with Lucy? What about your jealousy attacks?"

I am considering it. You want me to write a sexy, maybe even pornographic book?

"Well, you might get plenty of readers."

I don't want to go into such argumentation. I want to write whatever and however pictures and ideas emerge. Already certain ideas and events begin to link up. What is left unfinished will emerge. Yes, I wanted to write about my house and you interfered and put me on the defense again.

Ping-pong, ping-pong, ping-pong. Mind-fucking again. Actually I was a good ping-pong player, better than tennis. In South Africa I had a good partner, our housekeeper. She, with her husband and a boy with hair of carrot-color, lived with us for a while. The boy was not a great light but remarkable for his appetite. Asked what he wanted, he always answered: "Some more of everything."

We also had a nurse imported for the children. I believe she was engaged to someone overseas. She kept pretty much to herself, but when I took her along to the warm baths, she gladly and passionately made love with me.

Warm baths and hot springs: both mineral baths. The difference is that we have plunges 6 X 6 and 2½ feet deep, and they had 3 swimming pools with different temperatures. Well, one can't have everything.

To get there one had to travel over a hundred boring miles with one interruption, a waterfall. There was not much water. You had to go out of the car and pull a chain, which always reminded me of a magnified W.C.

The W.C. in my bathroom is a very ordinary john. But the bath! Everyone envies me. It is an oval tiled bath with steps leading down. Although I always wanted a large tub to lie in and to read comfortably in, this is not possible in this mammoth bath. It is at least six feet long, and to fill it we had to install a second heater. Several people can bathe together and sometimes we do just that, or maybe not just bathe.

"I see that you are now doing free associations."

Yes, and I don't feel too good about it *and* I feel good doing it. Like a seal, swimming, twisting, turning, diving through an ocean of words and facts. Not like sea-otters that swim in our bay, lying on their backs showing us how to open shells. Yes, I want to show you how to open your shell. No, I don't want to do it. I want to be left alone. Yes sir, No sir, yes, no, yes, no yes no yes no yesnoyesnoyesno.

"Maybe you are really crazy?"

No, just hungry.

"Fritz, you have to learn to discipline yourself."

Stop mind-fucking.

"Fritz, there is no need to use such obscene language. By the way, what do you mean by mind-fucking?"

We used to call it bullshit. This had some effect, but not its common use. "Mind-fucking," however, just because it's obscene, still has some shock-therapy value.

"Can't you use a more acceptable term?"

Yes. I can call it verbiage production, sentence ping-pong, bullshit, but what is the use? People who have surrounded themselves with thick verbal defenses will accept and argue with such terms and spew back sentences, but they themselves remain untouched. They are *about*ists.

"I am curious. Why do you select the bull as a representative for the animalistic defecation product?"

You might call it horseshit. I have no objection. I even classify those animalistic defecation products as symbols essential for the communication system of *homo sapiens*. How is this for a formulation? Would this kind of exact verbiage please you or put you to sleep?

"It might. What is your classification?"

a) chickenshit: small talk, exchange of clichés.

b) bullshit: rationalization, explanatoriness, talk for talk's sake.

c) elephantshit: high level discussion on religion, Gestalt Therapy, existential philosophy, etc.

"You seem to be biased in favor of c). At least you approach your task more scientifically now and begin to classify the verbal phenomena."

Now as you are appreciating me, I will give you another classification. 1) *aboutism*. 2) *shouldism*. 3) *isism*. Those are simple words. By adding "ism" to each of them we elevate them into the elephantshit class. By adding some high-sounding words, I'll make them acceptable to you.

Aboutism is science, description, gossiping, avoidance of involvement, round and round the mulberry bush.

"Why can't you stay serious just for a few minutes?"

O.K. O.K. You just gave an example of *shouldism*. I *should* be serious. Demands, demands, demands. The ten commandments. I demand this or that from you. If you don't comply, I feel frustrated and resent you. And *vice versa*. And the demands we are making on ourselves! And using the "why" as an excuse for a reproach attack!

Isism. A rose is a rose is a rose. "I am what I am, I'm Popeye the Sailor man." This is called the phenomenological or existential approach. Nobody can at any given moment be different from what he is at that moment, including the wish to be different. Tautology: the experience of self-evidence.

Moishe and Abe are playing cards.

Moishe: "Abe, you are cheating!!!"

Abe: "Yes. I know."

Fritz as an *about*ist, a storyteller; Moishe as a *should*ist; Abe as an *is*ist.

Now I can't resist
Even if it hurts
Be an aboutist
Play with bigger words.

Introjection and Projection
Retroflection, oh behold
Will not suffer more neglection
Wishing to be called.

Jump out of the garbage pail
Have a conversation
That the reader can avail
Himself of your location.

Introjection, what's your place?
Where are you located?
Retroflection? Well, it stays
Always self-related.

And Projection? You have been
Most despis'd and put on shelf.
You are more than just a screen,
Come, emerge, potential self!

RETROFLECTION
(INVERSION)

I AM AN ORGANISM
I WANT SOME FOOD

I WANT TO ATTACK SOME FOOD
IS THERE NO FOOD IN THIS WORLD?

THEN I HAVE TO EAT MYSELF UP

I ATTACK MYSELF, I TORTURE MYSELF

I KILL MYSELF

I FEED ON MYSELF

HELP! HELP!

(YOU-I) EAT ME UP

(YOU-I) WILL YOU
LEAVE ME ALONE

PROJECTION

I'M AFRAID OF YOU

YOU SHRUNK ME, COME BACK

YOU'RE PART OF ME

YOU PROJECTED ME

MY NAME IS NOW
PROJECTION

I'M NOW GOING TO TAKE YOU BACK.

I'M GOING TO RE-OWN YOU.

I'M HEALING
THE SEPARATION.

YES, BUT DON'T
JUST TAKE ME IN.

DON'T JUST
INTROJECT ME.

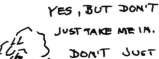

INTROJECTION

I'M AN INTROJECT. I'M A STRANGER
IN YOUR SYSTEM. I HOPE YOU CAN'T
STOMACH ME AND
LEAVE ME INTACT.

ON THE CONTRARY! YOU HAVE GOOD SUBSTANCE.
I'M GOING TO CHEW YOU UP AND ASSIMILATE YOU.

I'M MAKING YOU MYSELF
SO THAT
I CAN GROW.

Lecture on assimilation

It is my opinion that. . .

We have now to consider the fact that. . .

I shall now direct your attention to the following phenomenon. . .

"Are you collecting curtain raisers?"

Something of that sort. You know something? I was, up to

about fifteen years ago, too self-conscious to speak without a script. Today I don't bother with one even if I speak at a convention or have to address 1000 people.

In 1950 I went to Los Angeles for a short period. There was a tiny college "Western College for Psychoanalysis" or something like that. It had a double significance for me. Because of my books, I received an honorary doctorate in philosophy. I believe it was the only degree they ever gave. The other was that I discovered what self-consciousness was and overcame that very quickly.

"Many people suffer from that. Can you help them within a short paragraph or is it a trade secret?"

Not at all. Actually it is the mildest and most widespread form of paranoia. Self-consciousness is somewhat different from stage fright, but often interwoven with it. The term "self-conscious" is misleading; it should be called "critical-audience-conscious." The speaker is not really aware of his audience, which for him becomes a blurred unit.

This blurred audience becomes a projection screen. The speaker imagines the audience to be critical or hostile. He projects his own criticism on them, instead of observing what is really going on. He also projects his attention on them and feels himself as a focus of attention.

The cure is simple: Identification with the projection. Be critical of the audience. Pay attention and observe reality. Wake up from the trance of catastrophic expectations.

This, then, is the first example of projection.

We have come across retroflection or inversion a few times. Kierkegaard, an early existentialist, speaks of the relation of the self to the self. And this is exactly what retro-flection, bending back, is. The communication does not go from self to other, or from other to self, but from self to self.

Suicide, self-torture, self-doubt are good examples. The cure: Do unto others what you are doing to yourself.

"This sounds horrible."

It is not as horrible as it sounds. Actually it is sufficient, even required, that you do those bad things to the other in fantasy and psycho-drama. In any case, a person who tortures himself in your presence tortures you at the same time.

Once I slipped up very badly. A colleague asked me to have a session with a suicidal patient of his. I consented and we found out quickly that she wanted to kill her husband. And she did.

"So your therapy can be dangerous?"

Yes. Very rarely though. I have not seen much damage, but plenty of benefit for those hundreds of people with whom I have had a quick therapeutic encounter. I learned a lot from that case.

"How are you preventing such setbacks?"

I usually tell the group that I am not taking any responsibility for anyone except myself. I tell them that if they want to go crazy or commit suicide, that if this is their "thing," then I would prefer it if they would leave the group.

I also learned to be very sensitive to severe pathology. If somebody brings a dream of desolation with no people, no vegetation, or if he shows signs of bizarre behavior, I refuse to work with him. Usually I am then attacked for my cruelty and unwillingness to be "helpful." In those short weekend seminars I just have no time to get in touch with those shut-off people.

"And you did not spot this in the killer case?"

No, on the surface there was no gross pathology. Later I heard and understood her case from the introjection point of view. Her dybbuk was her mother who had killed her husband and got off scot-free. Perhaps she expected the same.

"Then you agree for once with Freud? Or do you also have to attack him for his projection and introjection discoveries?"

I fully agree with his projection theory. Only we are going now much further. We include most of the transference and very many memories, and, most important, all dream material. Freud's introjection theory is a horse of a different color.

"How can a theory be a horse?"

Shut up.

"You said a person living in the *now* is automatically creative. You bring a stale metaphor."

You are right. This is an introjection. This is foreign material.

"Then you don't like horsemeat?"

?

"You have said often that any metaphor is a mini-dream."

Like "A thought *hit* me" is aggressive. Right? How can a thought hit?

"And you don't like Freud's horsemeat?"

Oh, I see your point. I can't stomach his theory of introjection? Is that it? No. On the contrary. I chewed it very thoroughly and came to some interesting conclusions:

a) It is an organismic concept. You take in, ingest something, real or in fantasy.

b) Total introjection. You take in a whole person. The dybbuk. You can't swallow that person in reality: This has to be done in fantasy. This is the stage of a suckling, of the gulper.

c) Partial introjection. You take in parts of the person: mannerisms, metaphors, character features. This is the stage of a biteling, one who uses his front teeth.

d) Copying. This is not an introjection, but a learning and imitation process.

e) Destruction, the task of the molars. Freud overlooked this decisive stage. By de-structuring the mental or real food, we assimilate it, make it our own, make it self as part of the growth process.

f) We don't introject the *love* object. We take in the person who is *in control*. This often is a *hate* object.

g) Go back to the discussion of *ego* and *I*. The healthy *I* is not a conglomeration of introjects, but an identification symbol.

h) Aggression is not a mystical energy, born out of a death instinct. Aggression is a biological energy needed for biting, chewing and assimilating foreign substance.

i) Freud's *working through* demand is the equivalent of chewing.

j) Aggression can be sublimated into fights and wars.

k) l) m) n) to be filled in by a creative reader.

I am in real trouble. I am producing sentences on paper, having them typed, xeroxed, proofread. And all the time I don't even know to whom I am talking.

I am anxious to get some feedback.

When I am "thinking," I am also in fantasy. I talk to somebody and I don't know to whom I am talking. I don't really hear myself thinking, except in verse.

Sometimes I feel different. When I split myself up into topdog and underdog, I feel some communication. When I am playing a lecturer and demonstrate my theories, I am addressing a class. When I am attacking somebody, be it Freud or the Prussian lieutenant, I have a reader as witness of my courage and viciousness. In either case I am not alone.

When I am writing these sentences I am alone and . . .

Just now I had a sudden experience. I was dictating those sentences to myself, and I am also the recorder who has to watch grammar and spelling.

I can conjure up purposes and other justifications: to write a book, to exhibit myself, to satisfy the curiosity of my friends, to sort myself out. I am still alone and lost.

Where are you? Who are you to whom I want to speak? No answer.

I can't stop, either. I can't let go of the idea that I am doing something important for you and for myself.

If somebody were there, would he be interested? I used to boast compulsively to impress people with my brilliance; this is very much less now. And when I am impolite and rude, I also want to impress with my impoliteness and rudeness.

I would rather touch and kiss than talk. Am I playing true confession games? All those silly questions!

A fool is waiting for an answer.

I want to try the projection game. Mr. X, I want to show you how brilliant I am and I want to show you how evil I am.

Now, my reader, that is (I-you) am (are) not convinced of either and I try and try for seventy years to convince (me-you) that (I-you) am (are) brilliant and evil.

Hermann Hesse, Goethe, Mozart found a way out. They project the good and the bad into a novel, a play, an opera. Goethe did not admit to himself that he was the seducer, the all-negating spirit, the seeker of omnipotence, the counterpart of the angels. He puts it on Mephistopheles.

Mozart, or his librettist, does not admit to bragging about his conquests, his cowardice, his bribability. He puts it on Leporello.

Hesse does the same in the Steppenwolf, but he is also Siddhartha, the saint. Mozart's Don Giovanni can be the epitome of charm and courage, Faust the noble seeker of truth.

I got some consolation from those paragraphs. Or did I play a trick on you and myself by picking out brilliance and evil?

I am looking at you, my reader, with questioning eyes. My heart is heavy, lest you will throw me into your garbage pail.

Pride and confidence, where are you? Am I addressing you? Is my show of being securely grounded in myself a phony synthetic role? Does my smoking hide my unsureness?

These ruminations might bring me closer to investigating the smoking sympton, but I still don't know to whom I am talking.

> To whom to talk?
> I have no choice.
> With whom to walk?
>
> A whimper voice
> That is alone
> And is not found.
>
> They all are gone
> No noise.
> No sound.

The fact of talking is the message. True as far as the voice is concerned. The voice is the message. Persona, *per sona*, through sound. Per = through. Sona = sound, sonare, to sing. Try talking gibberish. Relieved from squeezing abstract notions into sounds, your voice gets angry or wailing or crushing or anxious.

Relieved from abstract notions I want to squeeze the sound into a loving potion. Looking, no listening, scanning for sound relations to sound, so that I can finish the verse.

Sound relations also mean healthy relations.

That is true, said he, snapping his fingers.

That is true, says I, lighting another cigarette.

I am getting through the impasse. I am listening to your voices. I have a sound relationship.

Do you sing, or do you saw?

Do you stroke, or do you rasp?

Is your voice dead, or soaked in tears?

Are you machine-gunning me with the rapidity and explosiveness of each of your words?

Do you put me to sleep with lullaby softness?

Do you take my breath away with the and—and—and—of your anxiety?

Do you scream at me, a shrew talking to a deaf neighbor over the fence?

Do you torture me with mumbling low sounds in order to make me strain and come to you to receive your mindless communications?

Or keep me on tenterhooks with stuttering, like telling endless jokes for just a tiny punchline laugh?

Is your voice boomingly filling the room, leaving no place for anyone else?

Or are you whining, whining, whining, turning me into your wailing wall?

Do you arouse tensions with elevated brows underlining a conspiratory whisper?

Do you punish me with the daggers of your Sunday-school teacher's finger-pointing screech?
Drown me with a priest's oily suffocation?
Or are you engulfing me in loving sound vibrations,
Melting me and turning on lush, embracing fantasies?

No need to listen to the content.
The medium is the message.
Your words lie and persuade
But the sound is true—
Poison or nourishment.
And I dance to your music or I run away
I cringe, or am attracted.
And get a consolation
From this investigation:
I myself can't be too evil, for many of you
Are in love
With my voice

And I found
My rhyme to *sound*.

Yesterday I had to give away a bride. Ben got married. Peter and Marya want me as the godfather for their child. What is happening to my "bum" image?

The ceremony is taking place next to the swimming pool. It is one of the extra-beautiful days of Big Sur. The sun is just a bit too warm. Everyone is dressed in their psychedelic Sunday best. I am wearing a white embroidered Russian shirt, a present from Jennifer Jones. Walking down through the deep thick lawn is like going through a mini-morass. Every step is heavy. Brave Marya. She is highly pregnant but keeps her chin up walking through dozens of camerashots.

This is my first function of this sort. I am oscillating between deprecating the ceremony as a routine performance with the (I believe atheistic) minister evoking the name of God as an empty eternity, and being moved by Ben's difficulty of overcoming his emotion while reciting his vow. He really seems to believe in his commitment.

The minister is unpretentious with a quiet good humor. The simplicity of the ceremony, although carried through with ritualistic exactitude, gives us a feeling of reality.

A couple of months ago Ed Maupin got married with the same sincerity, but—

Alan Watts performed the Zen-inspired ceremony—and I mean *performed*. He stole the show, which was hovering between the sublime and the ridiculous. It was a facsimile with fake and improvised props. Even the couple to be married seemed to be props and not the center of the occasion.

I love Alan and his frank admission, which adds to his mission, of being an entertainer. Seldom has anyone spoken so elegantly and so generously about the *non*-verbal. Ladies of all ages with higher ambition for redemption swoon before his wisdom. He has exquisite taste. In ancient Rome he would be in the high brass bracket of an *arbiter elegantiarum*.

Dear Alan, one day you will believe in your teaching. The wisdom of your intellect will enter your heart and you will *be* a sage, not just play one. You will be here not for the glory of Alan, but for the glory of no-thingness.

Ben is one of the left-overs from the second Esalen residential program. In a way he is also the savior of Esalen, though any resemblance to Christ is purely accidental. When Esalen went through a crisis and seemed to fall apart, he took over the management and put the right people in the right places.

The first program was rather ill-fated. The program director was Virginia Satir. She did not fit that role. She was not "the right person in the right place," which is the basis for any society or community's well-functioning.

Virginia, you have my love and my unstinted admiration. In many respects we are alike. Restless Gypsy. Greedy for success and recognition. Not willing to settle for mediocrity. You are a big woman with a big heart. Eager to learn. Fantasy for things to come. Your greatest asset is that you make people listen. You suffer, like me, from intellectual systematitis, but what you think and what you do don't come quite together. Too much explanatoriness.

You have projected your need for an understanding family, and, correspondingly, are family-phobic for yourself. Your dreams to settle down remain dreams. You wanted a house, bigger than mine, at Esalen. An unrealized dream. You wanted to be the director of the Esalen Program. Another dream gone haywire.

I admit, as a whole, the first year Esalen bums were a poor crop. Mostly escapists or shithorses. They came as strangers and remained strangers. They expected the staff to wait on them and they expected to be "processed." I don't know if anybody else could have done better, but they definitely felt abandoned when, after two weeks of intense therapy, you left them.

One of the left-overs from that crop was Bud who became the manager for a while. The staff and especially Selig did not take to him. They saw his management more as need for power and control than as an involvement as one of us. When he left, through false economy or whatever the reasons were, Esalen was close to bankruptcy. Then the second year residents stepped in and really put their shoulders to the wheel. They and John Farrington, our accountant, got Esalen through the financial impasse.

The other left-over was Ed Maupin. He was made co-director of the second-year program. I disapproved of having this meditation-addicted chronically embarassed unrealist taking on such a difficult task. Lately, however, I am beginning to revise my opinion. He is growing. He is applying himself and he is beginning to be in touch, and to discover his *Umwelt*(OZ).

I was glad to hear that Bill Schutz was to be in command. And I mean in command. He is something of a Prussian Officer, but he is also observant and skillful. He is an intellectual sponge, but deep inside suffering and desperate for growth. He tries to be hippish, but is more of a square. If he does not feel observed he looks somewhat morose. No wonder that he wrote a book on Joy, the usual psychiatric externalization.

Basically he is of good will and this is what counts. He put himself out to organize and to make a success of the residential program. And he did. From this crop emerged a number of beautiful people who are identifying themselves with Esalen. The wall between them and the staff is gone. Besides to Ben and Diana my love goes to John and Anne Heider, both of them extremely sensitive and beautiful. Also to strong and real Stephen and unpretentious, intelligent and loving Sarah.

Half an hour ago Neville, a South-African radiologist and I were reading the manuscript. He adores me and this is no wonder. The four-week workshop has done more for him than ten years of Reichian therapy.

He saw it first. Outside the window, apparently attracted by the light, hunched a racoon, the first one I ever saw, looking in with large brown eyes, unafraid of us.

Now that the bushes around the house are growing denser, I am getting more visitors. My favored one is a hummingbird hovering and darting right in front of the window. Today I discovered three small birds. They did not fly like hummingbirds, or have they not yet learned their helicopter tricks?

Cats walk by aplenty. One day last summer T.J. was lying on the deck in agony, apparently dying. T.J. is a venerable old tomcat, the head of the clan. With great effort he inched himself towards the edge of the deck. I went to fetch Barbara, Selig's girl, our mother of animals, but T.J. was gone. I saw him again later proudly sitting on the windowsill, never begging but graciously accepting food that is to his liking. Not like greedy cats, those youngsters that crawl all over you and the table to the dismay of guest-protecting waitresses.

Selig has a veneration for life in every form, which I don't quite share. Once we had a big rattlesnake in our unfinished stone wall. I killed him. When Selig arrived he was disgusted with me.

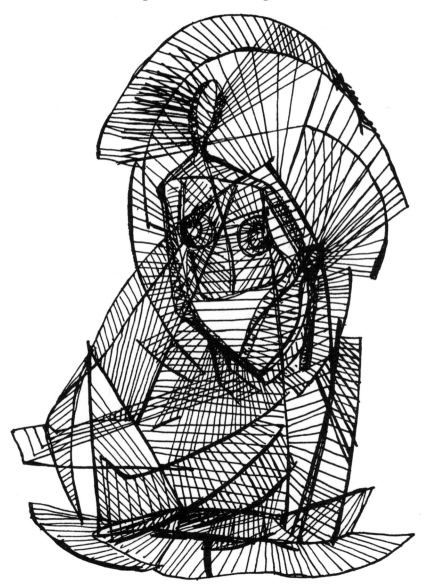

One of my prized possessions is a wire sculpture "Madonna with child" done by him. I first had her on the deck where you look at her and through her against and into the blue sky. One day a storm blew her overboard, down the steep slope. One of my seminarians rescued her with what seemed to me a risk to his life. Selig repaired the madonna and she stands now (opposite a medieval prophet, bought in Vienna) securely inside on the right upper sill of my center room, the room where I hold my workshops. Old bridge timber fanning out from the entrance to the glass front. The ceiling, also rising higher to the front, is used for pictures and a wire sculpture loan from Selig.

I wonder why people use only walls for hanging pictures.

Seminars of mine are conducted down in the lodge, workshops in this room. Weekend seminars are now my contact with non-professionals and they are, like all my "appearances," much in demand and oversubscribed. Still I admit now 70-80 people. I call those weekends my *circus*.

You would not expect that with so many in one weekend anything could be achieved, but on the contrary. I do some mass experiments, but mostly restrict myself to working with a single person in front of the audience. For my performance I need:

1) My skill
2) Kleenex
3) The hot seat
4) The empty chair
5) Cigarettes
6) An ashtray.

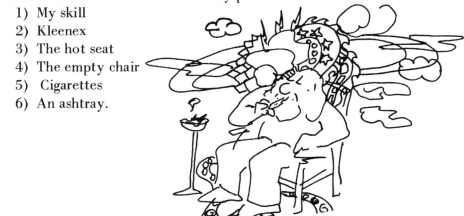

My skill: I believe that I am the best therapist for any type of neurosis in the States, maybe in the world. How is this for megalomania? The fact is that I am wishing and willing to put my work to any research and test.

At the same time I have to admit that I cannot cure anybody, that those so-called miracle cures are spectacular but don't mean much from the existential point of view.

To complicate matters still further, I don't believe anyone who says that he wants to be cured.

I can't give it to you. I am offering you something. If you want, you can take it. You are, as Kierkegaard said, in despair, whether you know it or not.

Some of you make the long journey to Esalen and might spend hard-earned money just to sneer at me, to show that I can't help you, to make a fool of me or to demonstrate my impotence to produce instant cures.

What does such an attitude do for you? Does it make you bigger?

I know that you are doing this to a hidden part of yourself, that you don't know *me*, that I am only a convenient projection screen.

I don't want to control you; *I* don't have to prove my authority; *I* am not interested in fighting.

Because I don't have to do this, I *am* in control. I see through your games, and, most important of all, I have eyes to see and ears to hear. You don't lie to me with your movements, your posture, your behavior. You don't lie to me with your voice.

I am honest with you, though it hurts.

I play with you, as long as you play roles and games. I mock your cry-baby tears.

I weep with you if you mourn, and dance with your joy.

When I work I am not Fritz Perls. I become nothing, no-thing, a catalyst, and I enjoy my work. I forget myself and surrender to you and your plight. And once we have closure I come back to the audience, a prima donna demanding appreciation.

I can work with anybody. I cannot work successfully with everybody.

The weekend setting is a demonstration seminar with volunteers who come up to the platform. And many of you scramble for an encounter, and many others learn vicariously. Some are closed-up and disappointed, but far more take something home. For the problems are few with many variations.

To work successfully I need a tiny bit of goodwill. I cannot do anything for you, my smart aleck.

In this short weekend I will not touch you, if you are deeply disturbed. I would stir up more than you can handle by yourself.

In this short weekend I will not open up to you if you are a poisoner who will leave me limp and depleted—incapable of attending to those who don't deserve the hate and disgust which I would carry over.

If you are a bear-trapper, sucking me in with "innocent" questions, baiting me, waiting for me to make the "wrong" move that will allow you to decapitate me, I will let you bait me, but avoid the trap. You will have to invest more until you are willing to surrender and to be yourself. Then you don't need me any more, or anyone else for your scalp collection.

If you are a Mona Lisa smiler and try to hide from me your indestructible "I know better," and expect me to wear myself out to get to you, I will fall asleep on you.

If you are a "driver-crazy" I will soon stop following you and arguing with you. You are a relative of the poisoner.

Kleenex: To cry at Esalen is a status symbol. "A boy does not cry" has been replaced by "Have a good cry," but—

Crying is not crying is not crying.

I don't know how many forms of tear production exist. I am sure one day someone will get a grant for a tear research to cover the whole range from the heartbreaking sobbing of a mother who has just lost her only child, to the phonies who can switch on their tears at will. I've seen a fiancé of one of my students domineer him with this well-developed gimmick.

Anyone whose intuition is intact feels immediately the difference between genuine compassion-evoking grief, and a performance that produces in the onlooker nothing but cold curiosity.

Once I did this too, as a mercy-producing stunt. I don't remember the occasion. I knew that if I only could produce sympathy I would get leniency instead of punishment. I did not feel anything. In cold calculation I conjured up my grandmother's funeral in my fantasy. It took me a couple of minutes, but I made it. The tears came and I got off the hook.

I learned in college to include a salt-free diet when prescribing bromides as a sedative. This could mean that salt might be an agent of the excitement metabolism and that crying is a de-salting process.

Its quieting and soothing result is a bromide-like medication. A "good cry" relaxes, and children cry themselves to sleep. I see authentic crying mostly as both a melting re-adjustment and a call for help.

I have not cried my heart out too often, maybe one or two dozen times in my life. These occasions were always peak experiences of being deeply moved—of grief, and at least once of unbearable pain.

I love the soft crying that goes along with melting. Very, very often the melting of a stubborn armor and the emergence of authentic feelings in my group turns me to loving surrender. Sometimes there is a chain reaction of the whole group, when crying becomes as infectious as laughter.

I love tearjerkers in the movies if they are credible at all. Occasionally, I must admit I shed tears even at sloppy sentimental crap, but most of all if somebody is transcending average human kindness, if he is too good to be true.

I love being sad without unhappiness and even love the embarrassment that goes along with it, as if I am caught indulging in a forbidden weakness.

One of my two deepest meltings was the despair outburst at the Arden house after my trip around the world. I could not say what was melting. The barrier between me and other humans? My hatred for lack of recognition? The thick skin I had acquired in the trenches? Or shall we be semantic and recall that despair is *désespoir*,without hope? Hope certainly was reinstilled.

The other occasion came during Lore's and my first visit to Germany after the second world war. I wanted to check out on both my deep hatred against Nazi Germany and a possible change of spirit there.

We had bought a second-hand VW in Paris which turned out to be a first-class bargain. I don't remember the exact figure, but I think I paid about $600 for it; we drove it for two months in Europe, three years in the States, and sold it for $700.

Anyhow, we entered Germany with that car at the Dutch border. We were not very encouraged. The customs officers exhibited the old German crudeness. We drove down along the Rhine. The atmosphere and our mood began to change somewhat. We went to Pforzheim, Lore's birthplace, and were made welcome. We visited the grave of Lore's father and I had a grief explosion.

And I mean an explosion. Unexpected, taken completely by surprise as if some boil had broken open. Lore cried somewhat too. I saw her curious, not-quite-understanding-what-is-going-on eyes through the mist during the moments I regained touch with the world. I felt close to her.

I don't understand the outburst either. My father-in-law and I were never close. As a matter of fact, if I was a black sheep for my family during my puberty years, I was a pitch-black-monster sheep for the Posner family. They did not trust me at all.

"I guess you are now going off on a spiel with the Posner family and dodging your operations again?"

So what shall I do?

"Decide once and forever to finish a theme."

Decidere, to cut off. The semantic significance is clear.

"Stop throwing that semantic sand into my eyes."

I was afraid you would say that semantic shit. It is not becoming to a topdog of a better-class Jewish family like the Posners to use such common language.

"I see you want to sneak the Posners in again by a generalized association."

Yes, I could have said the Goldens, and this would have brought us to Miami. That's the beauty of free associations; you can twist them into any direction. No better vehicle for phobic behavior exists.

"Well, have the Posners anything to do with crying or have the Goldens?"

Lore can easily cry when she is unhappy. I have never seen her abusing her tears. Of course she cried vehemently when Liesel, her sister, and her child were killed. They had managed to go underground in Holland and were caught by the Nazis shortly before the war ended. My impression was that Lore mourned more for her niece than for Liesel. She never could get herself to see the picture: *The Diary of Anne Frank.*

"I am sorry I was a bit rough on you. What about the Goldens?"

I invented that name to build a bridge to Miami.

"Was there any peak experience in crying?"

There certainly was. Oh, I don't mean the usual type of being moved. I don't even remember crying when I was so unhappy with Marty. I remember very vividly my crying with agony and pain before the second operation.

"Are those the suicide-substitute operations?"

When Faust gets upset with Mephistopheles he calls him a travesty of dirt and blood, a shithouse, as we would say.

The merry-go-round starts up again. Flashbacks aplenty.

The pleasure I took in my *bad* years playing and imagining myself Mephistopheles.

Aunt Schindler. A huge fat woman with the warmest all-loving heart, enjoying my performance. She is the only one taking my side: "He'll be all right."

My father's brother dying of rectal cancer. A bed of shit and blood. Disgusting.

My bed in Miami full of blood. Marty harnessing disgust, cleaning up efficiently. A final test of torture. Will she love me in spite of such ultimate ugliness?

I was always ashamed of being sick. It was like a stigma. Even in the trenches I preferred to conceal a high-fever tonsillitis than to admit to such "weakness."

I am now ashamed to admit to my bleeding piles and the soiled underwear that went with it.

That night in Miami when I woke up in that hemorrhage, I felt not ashamed. I felt calm, curious, and disappointed that I did not bleed to death.

I decided on an operation. Waking up the following morning, a male voice, a nurse, said to me: "Am I glad that you are back." I heard that I had spent 12 hours in the recovery room and that they had about given up on me.

What had happened? Wrong medication? A heart infarct? That would explain the heart trouble of the next five years. I had one vague recollection of wanting to reach for something; a nurse pushing me back.

The recollection of that night came back during a psilocybin trip. That was an uncanny recall of my fight against death. Going under, straining and waking up a bit, going under and coming up until finally, not unlike the dream of 1917, the will to live won out. And I came back from that trip with a strong will to live. Not to please someone, but finally for my own selfish sake. The existential mood of being "condemned to" life changed into being "blessed with" life. I completed the despair explosion that I had started in the Arden house.

I am blessed with life.
I am blessed with a full and useful life.
I am alive.
I am.

"But the operation itself was successful?"

Very.

"You spoke of a second operation."

Yes, I had another one within two weeks time. A few days after the discharge from the hospital I woke up in the early night with great pain in my bladder. I could not urinate. The pain increased and increased. If there ever was a superlative I have to use it now. In agonizing despair, with tears aplenty, I screamed, peculiarly enough, "Oh mama mia, mama mia." I suffered until daybreak. Another peculiarity. It never occurred to me to call a doctor immediately. Was it that I was afraid to (?) intrude, meeting an angry face, getting scolded?

Blessed relieving catheter. Diagnosis: enlarged prostate. Treatment: removal.

This time dozens of tests and examinations. One x-ray said part of the large intestine dropped. Should have another operation later. I had had enough of the surgeons. I never bothered and "it" never bothered me.

So they cut out the prostate and sterilized me in the process. I liked that idea and I liked the compliment: "We never had an M.D. who was such a good patient."

The time after that operation is in fog. I know that I went from Miami to Columbus and came back again. It feels as if that was an interruption prior to those operations, but I am not sure. Marty visited me there and helped me to organize a household. So it is likely before that time.

Here in Esalen are quite a number of men to whom I feel warm and loving. I don't know if it is that the atmosphere attracts that special kind of person to whom I can relate, or that my capacity for love has increased.

The friends I had in my earlier and later youth were always boys to whom I could surrender. The friendships after the first war and in South Africa were never deep enough to lead to full mutual trust. Here in the States I trusted Paul Weiss and I trusted Vincent O'Connell. Vince is somewhat twisted in the direction of the mystic. He is close to being a saint: extremely sensitive and perceptive. Being childless, he and April have adopted a flock of children and seem to make a good job of it.

He was chief psychologist at the Columbus State Hospital, and this is where I went as an instructor. I did not mind the job; I minded the 9 to 5 routine and left after nine months. This was a mistake as it soon became apparent. I should have stayed for a whole year. By chance I heard later that I could possibly have my German degree recognized in the District of Columbia. I applied and was rejected on account of the missing three months.

Now I am a non-psychiatrist in California, which does not

bother me very much as I am not prescribing any medicine and merely using, as a Commissioner of Mental Health revealed to me, my right of free speech: a redeeming feature of the American Constitution in contrast to its impossible demand: the pursuit of happiness.

"Then you don't believe in the pursuit of happiness?"

No. I think that this is a fallacy. You cannot *achieve* happiness. Happiness happens and is a transitory stage. Imagine how happy I felt when I got relief from bladder pressure. How long did that happiness last?

"Do you think that happiness as a permanent state can ever be achieved by anyone?"

No. You can sit for fourteen years in the same yoga position or lie fourteen years on the same couch or be for fourteen years a do-gooder. It is impossible by the very nature of awareness to be continuously happy.

"But happiness is a matter of awareness. You can't be happy without being aware. Or are you becoming Freudian, saying: 'I am unconsciously happy'?"

Nonsense. Awareness exists by the very nature of change. If there is sameness, there is nothing to be experienced, nothing to be discovered. In behavioristic language there is no stimulus for happiness.

To make a program: "to pursue happiness" includes the paradox "the road to hell is paved with good intentions." It also implies that unhappiness is bad.

"Are you all of a sudden turning masochist? Are you going to tell me that unhappiness is good? Are you now subscribing to the Christian virtue of suffering?"

Please understand. I merely state that happiness for happiness'
sake will at best lead to prefabricated fun *à la* Disneyland.

Masochism is pain for the pain's sake. To seek pain and make a
virtue out of it is one thing, to understand pain and make use of
nature's signal is another.

"What does pain signal?"

"Pay attention to me. Stop what you are doing. I am the
emerging gestalt. Something is wrong. Pay attention!! I hurt."

The hot seat:

I am on the seat
For you to see.
I feel my heart's beat
And I feel me.

I see you watching
However I move
And I see you catching
Me in my groove.

I am in pain
I will not reveal:
My fighting in vain
My wish to conceal.

My ache is insisting
I'm running away
And keep on resisting
The price I must pay.

I got to do it
Though dying with fright.
I'd rather go through it
With the hope that I might

Become *real*.

For two days I had no urge to write, be it that a number of OZ events had to take priority, be it that I struck pay dirt through this writing.

The obvious follow-up would have been to talk about what I am doing with/to the person on the hot seat: the approach to the *now* and the *how*, to responsibility and phobic behavior.

Lately I got into the habit of *using* my tiredness rather than to *submit* myself completely to it and to fall asleep. Last night I could neither sleep nor did I feel the impulse to get up and do something. I could stay for a considerable time in touch with my schizophrenic layer. I connected. I was not like on an LSD trip, mainly knocking out critical observations and promoting and intensifying the figure/ground exchange, thus giving me the conviction of a meaningful experience. No, I contacted a layer of fractionized, scattered bits and pieces, like tiny introjects, foreign material. Many were physical sensations and pictures, but unconnected. The subvocal talking was still somewhat coherent, even somewhat less shadowlike than my usual way of thinking.

I was glad that my suspicion of a schizophrenic layer was confirmed and that I got a good glimpse of it.

Apparently this being in touch produced somehow—I have not the slightest notion how—a change. The leching compulsion got a real break. I could, a few times, just *be* in the baths, and look and let go, instead of scheming how to create an opportunity to touch and be touched sexually.

When asked about giving up smoking I usually answer: "I wait until my smoking gives me up." I am more and more convinced that I am on the right track. About three months ago I gave up my compulsive masturbation and practically nothing of it is left.

I see now the first break in my sexplay and I know that one day something similar will happen with my smoking.

Yesterday I gave Jim Simkin's second group a dreamwork evening. One case merits recording.

I worked on the dream of a middle-aged woman. She can't let go of her daughter and is driving her crazy with her clutching, up to the point of institutionalizing. She lives her daughter's life, is over-"responsible," continuously interfering. Then I did something new.

I have played being born with a number of people with umbilical cord fixations. This time I let this woman go through the process of giving birth to her daughter. There was or is no birth trauma involved, but a lack of realization of parting. It became more and more clear that she had a hole—a sterile void—where others have a feeling of self, personality, uniqueness, individuality or whatever you want to call it.

After the birth experience I got her in touch with her body and with the world—something that was missing before. In other words I started to change the empty void, that was filled with her daughter, into the beginning of a fertile void of discovering her own substance and worthiness. I saw her today and, as usual in such cases, she felt great relief and a beginning change.

This only underlines Virginia Satir's opinion, that we have to find the person who drives a patient crazy.

I also recently had some shifty financial deals that would have previously upset me to the point of revenge or taking action, or, at least a great deal of fantasy preoccupation. I can take this much better in my stride as something unpleasant, but not catastrophic. They can *now* do this to me.

Also something anastrophic that might turn into an important development.

I have a confession to make. Besides that garbage pail in which I find people, events, toys, theories, etc., I have another one that is truly fantastic. There I find daydreams of all sorts. I find sexual fantasies and megalomaniacal doers-of-good and doers-of-evil dreams. I find dreams of hope and dreams of despair.

One of my favored ones is that I am being made dictator of the world and occasionally I spend quite some time in working out in detail how I would go about ruling the world. Then in checking out I see that to have any man with common sense would be better than to have this fractionalized world going down the abyss of self-destruction.

My impotence to actualize any of this does not bother me. Fantasizing as a pastime is rewarding enough.

My favored fantasy now is to write a Gestalt manifesto, holding four propositions.

1) Gestalt kibbutz.

2) Kubie's proposition of a new discipline: Therapist-teacher-psychologist.

3) Splitting the universities up into teaching versus research units.

4) Splitting our society into fits and non-fits (from an inspiration by E. Dreykhos).

The nearest to actualization—

"Stop that immediately."

—is the Gestalt kibbutz idea.

"I told you to stop that and pick up some loose ends from before."

There is much excitement being created—

"You just want to get a plug for your kibbutz into this book."

Yesterday we got a promising offer. Hi you, I don't need a plug.

"Never mind. At least you hear me now. Listen! That

manifesto belongs at the end of the book or as an appendix. Go on with your six implements. Or with the cessation of your leching."

Have you gone crazy? Me giving up leching? I said the first break in the compulsiveness of leching occurred. Right now I am building up a new compulsion: this writing. It's already getting difficult to get a free playful morning in life today with hot baths and getting shampooed and massaged. I am really going to miss that in my New Mexico kibbutz.

"Fritz."

?

"I warn you! You are getting sneaky again."

All right. I give in. But I will not say more about classification of crying or hot seat experience.

"O.K. At least you are on the level now. What about the empty chair?"

I mentioned that before. The empty chair is a projection-identification gimmick.

I love those hummingbirds, the dancers of the air. I saw a lovely green one in the bushes around the baths.

"What have they to do with the empty chair?"

Everything. They are there. They are real. The empty chair is vacant, waiting to be filled with fantasized people and things.

"For instance?"

For instance put the empty chair into the empty chair. What would you experience?

"If I am an empty chair I would feel useless until someone sits on me and uses me for support. Huh..That's funny. I always thought I don't need anybody."

Now give me some person or item from a dream.

"I don't remember anything."

Put Fritz in that empty chair.

"Fritz, I don't remember any dream material. Fritz says you are lying. I just remember an attaché case."

Now sit in that chair and be the attaché case.

"If I am an attaché case I have a thick skin, carry secrets, and nobody is allowed to get to those secrets."

Now I am going off stage and you "write a script," this is my term for changing seats and carrying on a conversation.

> You are making me curious. I'd like to get hold of your secrets.

> You can't. You don't have the key to open me up.

> I am a key. I am strong and well made, but my functions are limited. I can manipulate only one lock.

Play the lock.

> Come key. I waited for you. Come open me up. Come inside me.

> We fit perfectly together. I can twist you at will.

What does the lock say?

> Thank you. I don't need you any longer. You can go into the garbage pail.

> You bitch.

> Where do we go from here?

Whom are you asking?

You, Fritz.

Put Fritz into the empty chair. I give you your own personalized Fritz. Call him P.F. You can take him home and use him any time, free of charge. There is the "instant Fritz."

> P.F., what shall I do now?

> What are you avoiding?

> Opening the attaché case. There is nothing there. I feel cheated, P.F.

> Look closer.

> Yeah. some scraps of paper. Donation of three cows. Donation for a craftshop. One cement mixer. One truck.

> What do you say?

I am through with the empty chair. I want to deal with you, Fritz."

What have I done now?

"You put in the donations for your Gestalt kibbutz. You cheat."

You are my projection, aren't you? You are me. We have no secrets from each other.

The following is a story of a double projection. A psychiatrist invented a simplified Rorschach test. He used three basic figures.

One day, examining a new patient he drew a triangle. What is this?

"This is a tent. In this tent is a couple that's fucking."

Then he drew a rectangle. What is this?

"This is a big bed. Two couples are lying there fucking."

Then he drew a circle. What is this?

"That is an arena. There are a dozen fucking couples."

You seem to have a lot of sex on your mind.

"But doctor. You drew the pictures."

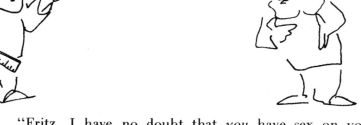

"Fritz, I have no doubt that *you* have sex on your mind. *You* introduced the story of the three basic figures. *You* saw the lock as a bitch."

You are right. *I* have sex on my mind. *I* introduced the story. *I* turned the lock into a bitch.

I am not willing to talk of the "fate of my libido" and put the responsibility on libido or the unconscious, as Freud does. I am also not willing to take the full responsibility for my sexual development.

I appreciate the Catholic outlook on sex as being in tune with nature. Sex and making children is an indivisible holistic process.

I was thrown into a world where that process was kept a secret from us and became a mystery.

I was thrown into a world where mind and body were divided things, and the mind became a mystery. An additional immortal soul produced a further complication.

I was thrown into a world where sex activity and procreation were divided, and sex turned into a matter of forbidden fun, sickness, and manipulation.

I was thrown into a family where children were not the deeply desired answer to two people in love.

I was confused by the knowledge I gathered in the gutter.

I was confused by Freud's pseudo-scientific sex theory.

I was confused by my ignorance of when sex was good and when it was bad, and when I was good and when I was bad.

I was most confused in my puberty years. Shall I blame my parents for lack of understanding, Ferdinand for seduction, myself for being "bad?"

I was "good" for many years until I slowly turned "bad."

It took me many years to come to an understanding of the problem of morals, and it was once more that the organismic outlook provided clarification.

Up to the age of nine I was given much appreciation. My grandparents used to say, "He is made from such stuff that gathers love from God and Man."

I must have been a lovable child indeed. Affectionate, eager to please and to learn. Long curly hair, to be sacrificed for school under protest and tears.

I could read very early. There were no books in my parents' home with two exceptions. My father had a library, locked away in his room. That room was a mystery. I like to think that my bad days started with my breaking in and exploring that room. More likely is that they began with my transition from the warm secure elementary scool to the strange, rigid atmosphere of the *gymnasium.*

In my grandparents' home I could find many books. I used to lie on the floor reading Mark Twain and many others.

Actually this collecting of memories in order to shed light on my childhood is contrived. I am scanning. I am not doing this for myself, but for an audience "as if" I am asked to write my biography, "as if" I should search, à la Freud, for explanations.

I am in Bob Hall's house, writing in the ironing room. I open an astrological book. I am a "Cancer" and read: "The moon gives desire to touch, to collect, it encourages curiosity and affects emotions strongly. It indicates ability to draw people towards you." How amazingly that fits. Add "a strong stubborn intellect" and you have covered much of my identity. Astrology, another mystery.

I am harping on the word "mystery." In my scanning a few minutes ago, I stopped short on several "mystery" incidents.

Besides my father's locked-away books, I had access to a "mystery" series, a weekly installment read by our servant girl.

My sisters and I were mostly close. Once I was excluded from a game they played in a courtyard, a boy standing guard. I suspected sex games. How I came to that suspicion I don't know. I only was sure something mysterious went on.

Closely connected with mystery is awe.

Religion and the goings-on in the temple did not produce any awe. I found it strange and peculiar what these people were doing, taking the prayer roll out of its sanctuary and reading in a strange language with peculiar movements and voice.

We had to learn Hebrew. Everything was impersonal with a few exceptions. For instance, their interest in my nose after an accident that is vivid in my memory.

We three children had passed a house being built when the wind blew a heavy fence over. The edge struck my nose and fell on Grete and broke her leg. The foreman ran about in despair, repeating his innocence; an ambulance took us to a first-aid station. I liked the excitement and fuss, but screamed when they put iodine on my wound; and I liked the fuss the rabbi made later inspecting my injury, for my nose was not even broken.

I liked the admiration and the presents I got at my *Bar Mitzvah* when everybody was proud of how well I had recited my prayer. There was even a present from the Staub family. For a few weeks I had a reprieve from my black-sheep status.

Perhaps the main incident by which I had acquired that status was my breaking into my father's secret room.

I had secured the key somehow, and when nobody was at home went into that room.

I found an indescribable mess. My father never allowed anyone to come in and clean up. There were shelves with books to be investigated. But what a disappointment. All of them were related to my father's hobby and ambition: to be a Grand Master of the Freemasons.

He loved to be called a "Speaker" and with the broad blue ribbon across his chest, a long impressive beard, a powerful figure, his was a magnificent appearance indeed.

He never made it to be Grand Master of one of the large established lodges, so he created his own. After a few years they usually blew up and he founded a new one as an audience for his performance and long speeches about ideals. The introduction into the lodge, as you might well know from the "Magic Flute," was supposed to be an ordeal through which a neophyte was to show his courage and worthiness to become a member of the secret sect.

When I was about eighteen and I had been through the impasse of my "bad" years, he decided that it was time for me to be introduced to his lodge. I was curious to penetrate the veil of that mystery and ready to go through that ordeal.

What a shame and disappointment! I was blindfolded. Two men led me through some halls and rooms, slammed doors, and I heard some noises that were supposed to be frightening. Later, some compulsive rituals. I had difficulties to keep a straight face and never returned to the sessions again.

At the parties, for instance Christmas, however, my father became his Rabelaisian self. He loved to dance the *krapolka*, to drink, to kiss. As a matter of fact, he chose as his profession to be a travelling salesman for the very excellent Palestinian wines. Of course, he was not a "travelling salesman," he was a "Chief Representative" of the Rothschild Company.

Once he made a remark which I resented deeply. "So what! I drink myself to death. My son will look after the family."

Basically I hated him and his pompous righteousness, but he also could be loving and warm. How much my attitude was influenced by my mother's hatred of him, how much she poisoned us children with it, I could not say.

My breaking into the secret room would not have had severe consequences had it not been for a complication: a piggy bank, that contained a gold piece which was supposed to be my sister Else's future property. I extricated that gold piece and with it I bought stamps for my handsome blond Christian friend, hoping to buy his friendship or as a token of my friendship. How many reproaches I got for that theft and how many times over I had to repay it!

When the theft was discovered, I ran away in terror. I slept on staircases in strange houses. I had no money. Then I visited some friends on the other side of Berlin, got food and car fare which I kept to buy some bread the next day.

Then I calculated: maybe "they" think that I killed myself and "they" would not send me to a reformatory as "they" had threatened so often. Maybe "they" might even be glad that I am alive.

So I returned and found a deeply frowning gathering, including

Uncle Eugen, my mother's doctor brother, another pompous ass. The verdict was my father's, "I'll forgive you (remember he was a Freemason and to forgive was an important function of that breed: cf. Mozart's beautiful aria for bass, my father's favorite song: "These sacred rooms hold no revenge for you") *but* I will never forget what you did to me." Neat, isn't it?

My position in the *gymnasium* was already deteriorating. The director had a Polish name, and possibly to prove his Aryan blood he was very, very nationalistic. The school was new and he gathered a staff that can best be described by paraphrasing Churchill: Seldom have so few teachers tortured so many children for such a long time. The basic attitude was discipline and anti-Semitism.

I failed in my entrance examination and was sent to a tutor who liked my intelligence and used this freely to play down my co-pupil, a dunce. Once I had shit in my pants on my way to him. Though I managed to clean off most of it in a public lavatory I must have been quite a stink. The tutor was sniffing during the whole session and was very mistrustful of the co-pupil. I did not say a word. This, I believe, was my first act of dishonesty. In the following years in the *gymnasium* I learned to lie quite successfully.

We were four Jews in our class. Krafft became a psychoanalyst. Schildkraut made a name for himself in the movies, and Hollaender composed many lovely songs for Marlene Dietrich.

When we got a demerit our parents were notified, postage unpaid. I was caught between my hatred for the school and the terror of my parents' scolding, until I found a way out: to wait for the mailman, intercept the school letter and forge my parent's acknowledgement. Finally I was caught in this, too. I drove my mother slowly, but surely, to despair. The great ambition of her life melted away; I became untamable, cut off the strings of her cat-o-seven tails. Once, running away from her grip, I locked the door, smashed the glass window of that door and made faces at her, enjoying her impotence to get at me.

In school I deteriorated so that I had to repeat the seventh-grade year and failed again and was kicked out of school. At that time in Germany it never occurred to anyone that the drop-out of a bright, warm kid might not be his fault alone.

The other drop-out was Ferdinand Knopf, my initiator to sex, whom I accepted easily as leader. We never masturbated each other, but simultaneously while he was telling me stories of his elder sister's adventures. I easily got an erection but was too young to have an emission. Then came my initiation to fucking.

We bought some candy bars (every step was his suggestion) and found a prostitute who seemed to care for him. We both were about thirteen years, but he looked older.

We took the local train to the Greenforest, very close to Berlin. They chatted all the time, I was apprehensive and mute. In the forest we promised not to peek. I bridled my curiosity. Then came my turn. The girl soon became impatient with my inability to have an orgasm and pushed me away. I turned around. Ferdinand was looking. I felt betrayed.

Soon afterwards, his leadership did something great for me.

After I was thrown out of school I became an apprentice to a soft goods merchant. I played pranks on the boss and was dismissed. Ferdinand was enterprising as usual and found another school for us, the *Askanische Gymnasium*, a liberal school. I passed the entrance examination, loved quite a few of the humanistically oriented teachers and wrote such good papers at the *Abiturium* that they dispensed with the oral examination.

This happened in spite of the fact that I had already begun my multiple life. Or was it on account of. . . ???

On my way to San Francisco, I stopped in Monterey for a panel discussion during the "Transactional Analysis" congress. I like the term "transaction," indicating that in a verbal interchange something real is happening, something more than the exchange of clichés, more than verbal ping-pong, more than the "who is right?" game. I like Eric Berne and I especially like Bob Goulding who was the mediator. I had a well-meaning young opponent who was no match for me. I was disappointed that Eric did not act as my counterpart.

I was always impressed by Eric's emphasis on role-playing, yet what I saw in my opponent was disillusioning. Not only did it look like a leaf from the Freudian approach, but like a denial of Eric Berne's own dictum that we are *playing* roles. The two roles I could observe were confined to parent and child and they were taken so damned *seriously*. The real game they play, the compulsive pigeon-holing of each sentence as belonging to either the child or the parent, remained unnamed. The idea of maturing, of integration and transcendence of role-playing seemed to be alien. Like with the orthodox analysis, the interest stayed with the middle zone. To be in touch with the world and oneself did not appear to be an integral part of my opponent's approach. Stroking is forbidden except symbolically.

I appreciate one of their games: stamp collecting. If you have a book of green stamps, you are entitled to feel ten feet tall; if you have a book of black stamps you are entitled to a depression, maybe even suicide.

Yet I am envious of Eric's success.
Yes, I am jealous I admit
(You have a perfect smeller)
That Eric's treatise was a hit—
A hundred week best-seller.

There should be something between the turning-on bit of the Schutzes and the Gunthers with their hundred gimmicks and the drabness and poverty of the two-role restriction of the Bernesians. Give me at least occasionally a prince who turns into an ugly frog.

I just realize that I left out an important merit of Berne's approach. Reich gave Freud's resistance notion a body, a piece of reality which he called the armor. Berne gave Freud's super-ego a tangible opponent, the child. Freud's super-ego domineers abstractions such as instincts, ego, actions. Berne thus established a true polarity.

I call these opponents topdog and underdog with emphasis on the control needs and resentments, demands and mutual frustrations.

I see those inner conflicts, like the conflicts between parents and children, husband and wife, therapist and patient, as attempts

—and usually successful attempts—to retain the status quo: to kill the future, to avoid the existential impasse and its pseudo-agony.

I see these conflicts subside, and integration and harmony take over, as soon as the opponents come to their senses, mainly to their ears. It is not a semantic gimmick to equate hearing and understanding. It is true communication.

The humility of *under*standing contrasts with the control needs of *over*standing, of righteousness.

Fighting is good if it mobilizes one's potential, as in many sports and intellectual competition. It is based on the joy of growing.

Fighting is bad if it is mobilized by prejudices and righteousness. It is based on the joy of destruction.

This is "good" and that is "bad." Judgements, morals, ethics.

Where do they come from? Are they parts of nature, the voice of God, the whims of lawmakers? What makes us attack the "bad" and idolize the "good?"

Up to the time of Nietzsche and Freud, the conscience was considered to be man's highest-valued inheritance. Kant still places the Categorical Imperative at par with the eternal stars.

Compare this with Hitler's cynical: "I can declare anyone enemy or friend at will."

The Catholic view that we are born in sin, with inadequate moral equipment for life, complicates matters still further.

As Darwin dethroned the role of man as being an extra-special divine creation unrelated to the animal, so did Freud debunk conscience as a divine institution. He made clear the intrusion of society, via papa and mama, into the human animal. He made clear the continuation of social taboos within the human being through the mechanism of introjection; of internalizing the policeman.

He is not quite ready to accept the human animal including sex for what it is. He has to justify it. There is still an undertone of the Catholic badness in his infant, including his projection of a polymorph perversity into the child.

"Can we go a step further and see the good/bad dichotomy as an organismic function?"

I believe we can. We can look upon that dichotomy as a projected organismic reaction.

"Do I hear correctly?
I believe you said
If we re-act projectly
We know good and bad."

That comes later. That is the reaction to the projected reaction.

"I find it amazy
What you said affirms
How you drive me crazy
With your pompous terms."

On the contrary. My honorable intentions are to drive you sane.

"You denied completely
Stimulus-reflex.
Now you sneak in neatly
Bring re-actions backs."

Bring reaction back, not backs.

"You reacted badly
To my little song.
Stated mean and sadly:
I am bad and wrong."

You are coming closer. If you hadn't disturbed me, I could have started to discuss "good" and "bad" as an organismic function, I might even have ventured into a strange land: The chemistry of morality.

"???????????"

Freud was a "placer." That is, he was topologically oriented. He pushed things around; he placed things. Though he reserved the term "displacement" for certain events, most of his theory can be understood in terms of movement in space. This sounds paradoxical. At first glance, Freud seems to be time-oriented, as his preoccupation with the past is obvious.

"Are you getting at Freud again?"

By no means. I am trying to get *to* him. You might say that I use him for my own understanding. I used topology in three forms (projection, introjection, and retroflection) for twenty-five years, definitively following Freud's way of thinking, while I was denying its validity in regard to other phenomena.

"Give us some examples."

Take "transference." It means literally to put one item from one place to another. That term has been obfuscated by giving it all kinds of connotations, like trust, fixation, demands for support, etc. Originally it means to transfer one's feelings from a father, etc., to the therapist. Later the term becomes woolly and methodologically a sleight-of-hand. Negative transference no longer means the change from credit to debit, but the display of negative, probably hostile, behavior.

Consciousness and "the" unconscious are places too. The unconscious becomes a place of things "mis"-placed. Mouth, anus, and genitals are locations for placing libido.

Freud's name for figure/ground is cathexis: *Besetzung*, sitting on, occupation of a place—only he attached some glue where the utmost freedom for change is desirable. In other words, process is neglected and upstaged by mechanical thinking.

Nowhere does this become as clear as in his introjection view. One moment the object is outside, and the next it is inside the organism. The mechanical process of grinding down is just hinted at and the chemistry is non-existent.

After the food has been ground down to a pulp, a further destructuring by the digestive juices is required. The food, mental as well as physical, cannot be used by the organism for its specific requirements unless it is broken down to amino acids, etc.—that is, to such elementary stuff with which the cells can cope.

This is the zero-point. This is the moment of assimilation, of changing foreign stuff into self. Up to this point, the organism deals with its needs, appetites, its minuses $(-)$.

The next step is the accumulation and disposal of chemical stuff which is unusable, which clogs up the works to the point of becoming poisonous and detrimental to the organism. Physiologically speaking, through the kidneys, liver, etc., a process of unpoisoning is taking place. To achieve zero, the organism has to diminish its (+) of undesirable substance.

Toxic people lack a well-functioning poison-eliminating system.

We are far from a true understanding of the relationship between—maybe the identity of—organismic behavior and personality behavior.

"I see you made some shortcuts *and* you got your chemistry in. I still don't see the connection of chemistry and morality."

I like the formulation that morality is originally not an ethical but an organismic judgement. Let's go back to my "bad" years. My behavior made my parents feel bad. They felt irritation, anger, disgust. They did not say, "*I* feel bad." They said, "*You* are bad," or at best, "You make me sick."

In other words, the primary reaction is projected and becomes a moral judgement. The next step is that certain forms of behavior are called "bad" by a community and even elevated to the status of "crime."

The same thing applies to the opposite. A boy who is out to please makes his environment feel good. Now he is labeled a "good" boy and entitled to praise, lollipops, and medals.

Conditioning, ego-boundaries, education, justice, change, projection, and some more phenomena are beginning to fall into their places.

I, you, parents, society, spouses say:
"I feel good in your presence, I feel comfortable.
I call you 'good.' I want you *always* with me.
I want you always to be like this."

I, you, parents, society, spouses say:
"I feel bad about you. You make me uncomfortable.
If you *always* make me feel bad, I don't want you.
I want to eliminate you. You should not be.
Where you are, there should be 'nothing' instead."

I, you, parents, society, spouses say:
"Sometimes I feel good about you and sometimes bad.
When you are good, I flow over with appreciation and love
    and let you share it.
When you are bad, I feel poisonous and punitive.
I flow over with revenge and hate and let you share my
    discomfort."

And we say: "We don't tolerate your changing from good to bad to good to bad to good to bad. We are going to change you, to condition you with reward and punishment. We educate you by reconditioning your good behavior until you, devil, turn into an angel, or at least into a facsimile of one, until you become what We, We, We, want you to be."

We shift the responsibility onto you. We lose our response-ability, *our* awareness of *our* discomfort. We make out that *your* behavior is responsible, that *you* ought to respond to our need. We blame you and we *re*act to you.

We may be all-accepting saints like Carl Rogers, or anger-bristling, gouty, crochety misanthropes rejecting any intrusion into our privacy. We might kill or imprison you if you show the slightest deviation from the party line. If you are bad, you have to be isolated until you repent and promise to be good. You will be sent to your room if you are a child, put behind locked doors if we call you a criminal or a psychotic, into a concentration camp if you oppose a dictator.

If you are good, we identify with you because you identify with us. If you are bad, we alienate you; you don't belong to us. If you are good, we are in confluence with you. If you are bad, we build walls between us. In neither case are we in contact. For contact is the appreciation of differences. Confluence is the appreciation of sameness. Isolation is the condemnation of differences. In short, the experience of good and bad regulates the structure of the ego-boundary.

Esalen is in a crisis again. The financial impasse has been overcome, but something more fundamental is at stake. Esalen has become the symbol, both in and outside the States, for the humanistic-existential revolution, for finding and promoting new ways for sanity, growth, and the development of the human potential.

Mike Murphy, over-anxious to give everybody an opportunity to "do his thing" and because of the need to stay financially sound, has not shown enough discrimination to keep out the weeds, or at least to prevent them from suffocating the flowers. Esalen's historical mission is at stake. Untrained youngsters lead encounter groups: "We turn on without LSD. To hell with diagnosing and tampering with borderline cases. To hell with disappointment-reactions when the promised 'self-actualization' fails to take place."

If the American middle-class people learn of the fact that they might become alive, if they come to sample opportunities to see that there is more to life than the production and taking care of things, fine.

But they come unprepared. They are afraid to speak up if they are told this or that gimmick or technique is the right way, and they become phony in a different way.

We are just beginning to discover effective means and ways of growth which can produce change. Will this be drowned in a wave of faddism and fashion that can produce nothing but a backlash? Will the phonies take over, or will the real and sincere people survive?

In contrast to the seminarians, most of the staff here are real people. They earn little money, but have the privilege of being themselves. Many of them are beautiful and lovable. Of course, some bad eggs and phonies get in too, but usually they are inched out sooner or later.

Without the staff, Esalen would not be that unique place it is. Never in my life did I love and respect so many people as I do here.

Besides Selig, I would single out Ed Taylor and Teddy as two of the few people in the world I trust unconditionally.

Ed is Barbarossa, the redbeard, a pianist and baker. I nearly wrote he baked the bread that made Esalen famous. I love to play chess with him. Most chess players are determined to win, compulsive computers, taking up much of my time, uptight haters when they lose, forgetting that we are playing a game.

Not so with Ed. We are playing. We have fun. To mate the king for us is just one of the rules of the game. Moves are not unretractable commitments. We reserve this for real life.

Teddy is a fine woman. This sounds somewhat stuffy. Let's rather say she turned into a fine woman. I know people use the word "fine" lightly. I use it seldom. Refined, finery. A good texture. Nothing gross about her. Boisterous as I am, I like the contrast of her unassuming way of being. Friendship with a dash of love, admiration and rather mute disapproval. With Teddy, I always know where I am.

I can't say the same about Lore. After all the years, I am still confused. We met over forty years ago, through Fred Omadfasel, who also worked at the Goldstein Institute.

She was the eldest of three. I liked her sister Liesel. When we met again in 1936 in Holland, we had some lovely encounters. Compared to Lore's heaviness, intellectual and artistic involvement, she was simple, beautiful, and flirtatious. The youngest was Robert, whom Lore apparently had, as a child, treated with contempt. Robert and I had a dislike for each other which we never overcame. When I first came to the States, alone, I lived for a short while with his family. It was, to say the least, very unpleasant, like a continuation of the seventeen years before in Germany when I was looked upon as an outcast who dared to intrude into the well-to-do Posner family.

Actually, it was the other way around. I tried several times to get away from Lore, but she always caught up with me.

I mentioned Lore's father before, who was fond of Lore, spoilt her, and let her always have her way. Her mother was a very sensitive woman, fond of her piano, hard of hearing, which was part of her withdrawal status. Lore disliked her deeply. I rather liked her and she liked me. She visited us in South Africa and insisted on going back, even on taking her valuable jewels with her, lest the Nazis be angry with her.

I don't feel good writing about Lore. I always feel a mixture of defensiveness and aggressiveness. When Renate, our elder child, was born, I was fond of her and even began to reconcile myself somewhat to being a married man. But when later I was blamed for anything that went wrong, I began to withdraw more and more from my role as a *pater familias*. They both lived, maybe still do, in a very peculiar clutching symbiosis.

Steve, our son, was born in South Africa and was always treated by his sister as a dunce. He developed in the opposite direction. While Renate is a phony, he is real, slow, dependable, rather phobic and stubborn in asking and accepting any support. I was moved when I got last Christmas the first personal and warm letter from him.

We have four grandchildren. No great-grandchildren yet.

Maybe one day I will feel like sorting myself out and will write about my voyeuristic compulsions centered around Lore, about her sometimes brilliant insights and her care for me when I was sick.

Right now it appears to me that we lived essentially parallel to each other, with relatively few peak experiences of violent fights and love, spending much of our talks in tedious "can you beat that" games.

Lore was, like many of our friends, opposed to calling our approach Gestalt Therapy. I thought of Concentration Therapy or such like, and rejected it. This would have meant that my philosophy-therapy would eventually be categorized as one of the hundred other therapies, which indeed to quite an extent has been done.

I was bent on the all-or-nothing position. No compromise. Either American psychiatry would one day accept Gestalt Therapy as the only realistic and effective form of understanding, or else it would perish in the debris of civil war and atomic bombs. Lore did not call me a mixture of a bum and a prophet in vain.

In 1950, Art Ceppos took a chance in publishing the book that was, like most of his publications, off the beaten path. He certainly gambled, and he gambled well. Sales of *Gestalt Therapy* steadily increased from year to year, and now, after eighteen years, it is still increasing in sales.

My prediction was that it would take five years to bring the title across, another five to get people interested in the content; five years more for acceptance, and another five years for a Gestalt explosion. This is about what is happening. My philosophy is here to stay. The crazy Fritz Perls is becoming one of the heroes in the history of science, as someone called me at the convention, and it is happening in my lifetime.

Two years ago, we barely managed to have one panel in the APA convention. Last year, I got a standing ovation. We had a moving 75th birthday celebration with a banquet and *Festschrift*, a collection of contributions to Gestalt Therapy, and a film by Dick Chase.

The paper of Joe Adams was a surprise for me. He lives in a house on the coast and is a rather shy, unassuming fellow. I never thought he appreciated me and my work; he never attended any of my seminars. And here is a very knowledgeable discussion of the immortals, and Perls has a place among them.

Another one was Arnold Beisser's paper that in style and content can be called a classic.

I have known Arnie for so many years. Hello, Arnie. It's good to be with you, if only in fantasy. I know we love each other, and yet we are hardly ever free from self-consciousness when we meet. You look so fragile in your chair. I never asked you how it feels not to be able to stretch your arms freely when you want to embrace somebody. What a courage to come to terms with life after being deeply involved with sports and then being stricken by infantile paralysis, barely managing to survive.

How are you doing in your training center? How is Rita? I want to tell you what an excellent paper you wrote. So few people understand the paradox of change.

I often thought I was not recognized because I was twenty years ahead of my time, but I see that you had a better perspective of the rapidly changing times.

When Clara Thompson suggested to me that I should become a training analyst in the Washington School, I declined. I refused to accept the notion of adjusting to a society which was not' worth adjusting to. As all schools preach adjustment to some point in history that is already past, they create merely lost souls.

I, we, create a solid center in ourselves; we become like rocks, with the waves flowing around us.

I know that this is a vastly exaggerated metaphor. You put your mark on your environment rather than reacting to it.

Thank you, Arnold Beisser, for your understanding, trust, and courage.

In working with a patient or whomever I meet, I am expecially alert to whether he wants to please or displease me, whether he wants to play the good or bad boy.

If he wants to displease me, control me, fight me, make fun of me, challenge me, I am not interested. As a matter of fact, I am in control because I do not try to control him. I may refuse to work with him. Often, after I have dismissed him from the hot seat—or on rare occasions, thrown him out of the group if he is too destructive—he usually comes back the next time with an astounding readiness to work. After all, there is a coward behind every bully, as there is a spiteful brat within every good boy.

The good patient, like the good boy, wants to bribe with his behavior. If the therapist is interested in childhood memories, he brings memories galore. If the therapist is problem-oriented he brings those, and if he runs out of problems he creates new ones. If experiences are demanded, he'll mobilize his hysteria and blow up his molehills to peak experiences. He'll give puzzles to the interpreter, swooning to the turner-onner, doubts to the persuader, and so on and on—anything to keep his neurosis.

We are back where we started from, the problem of identification. Do we identify with our true self or with the demands of otherness, including the demands of a self-image? These demands from the environment and introjects put us into a position of reacting rather than acting, expressing, outgoing. The adjustment theories give preference to the social demands. Many philosophies and all religions condemn the organismic needs as selfish and animalistic. The best solutions come about, of course, when the needs of self and society coincide. By society, I include parents, spouses, therapists, teachers, and hangers-on; the external society as well as the internal society, the introjects. The indecision of whom to please, oneself or the other, constitutes the neurosis conflict.

Both sides are full of danger. If we are on the side of the angels, we have to sacrifice, disown, alienate, repress, project, etc., much of our potential; if we identify with our needs, we might be punished, cast out, despised, left without external support.

The therapeutic solution is rationality, the realization that many of our catastrophic expectations have no validity, that many of the introjects are obsolete, only a burden. By getting in touch with environment and self, the patient learns to differentiate between his fantasies and his assessment of reality.

While the conflict between the individual and society is obvious and known to everybody, while the conflict between selling out to society and making one's own bed is nothing new, while the division between compliers and rebels remains unchanged throughout the ages, yet little is known of the internalizing of those conflicts, and how to go about finding an integrative solution.

Such a solution demands an understanding of the function of self-boundary and ego-boundary. Both are contact boundaries. The expression self-boundary is correct; the term ego-boundary is restricted to the individual, but its laws apply to all contact boundaries. These boundaries are determined by the identification/ alienation dichotomy. This investigation will hopefully lead us to the most important and most difficult phenomenon—projection.

I would like to interrupt this tedious abstract discussion by bringing in an example highlighting the relevance of our investigation.

A group of citizens is engaged in removing the separation boundary between black and white people. Usually, the freedom fighters identify with the plight of the Negro and demand the Negro's identification with their efforts. While they are engaged in such an integration process, another boundary is created, a dichotomy between the freedom fighters and the anti-freedom fighters.

During World War II, the boundary ran between the Allies and the Nazis, which soon shifted to a different boundary called the "iron curtain."

I could recite dozens of examples that such boundaries always exist between individuals, families, cliques, clans, nations, strata of society, and conclude that ideals like the United Nations and all-men-brotherhood are lacking perspective of the total situation and thus lead to foolish optimism.

In Durban we had an international club with Whites, Negroes and Indians. We got along fine with the Negroes and Indians, but all attempts to get the last two together failed.

The real boundary in the United States is not the split between Democrats and Republicans, or between management and labor, or between whites and minority groups, or law-abiding citizens and rebels.

The boundary is between "fits" and "non-fits."

I use those terms deliberately in order to avoid moral judgements such as good and bad or right and wrong.

In order to understand my ideas about a solution we have to realize that it would involve a plan of a magnitude like the multi-billion aerospace program, but the difference would be that rather than to use more money, it would in the end save many billions. What is more it can be carried out, or at least considered and started by any establishment in power.

I doubt however that in a technocratic society which is nearly unlimited in its "thing" planning, a humanistic enterprise of such magnitude could be understood. The only hope lies in the acknowledgement that we are *de facto* stuck with a humanistic problem of gigantic proportions with the explosive power of a potential open civil war.

With a small percentage of exceptions, every citizen belongs to one of these three categories:

a) The fits. They produce, trade, and service "things," and take care of the producers, traders and servicers of things. They are financially self-supporting and form a rather tightly-organized society.

b) The non-fits. This is a highly *dis*organized society and is falsely accepted as falling into many different and independent categories: the criminals, the lunatics, the drop-outs, the unemployed, the hippies, the poverty-stricken, the drug-addicts, the sick, the ghetto-dwellers. They are financially a burden to the fits, as they have to be supported or imprisoned.

c) The intermediate class, the caretakers of the non-fits. They are also paid and used by the fits. They include police, welfare workers, the staffs of hospitals and prisons, psychologists, doctors, ministers, etc.

What counts here is the idea, not minute details of who belongs where.

What counts is the resentment the fits feel for the non-fits, because of the huge amount of tax money to be spent on them.

What counts is the resentment and hate the non-fits feel for their dependency and lack of understanding.

The trend has always been to turn the non-fits into fits by cure, repentance and conditioning.

Make the non-fits self-supportive! Fits, understand coexistence!

At least look at the problem. Use your computers!

Make pilot studies. There should be somewhere a sociologist in the world who could take charge of a socio-space program. And, Generals, consider: concentration camps are not the answer.

Contact boundaries, recognition of difference, yes.
Walls, condemnation of difference, no.
Power or sanity?
Or:
the use of power
to restore sanity
would be
good.
But it will
as always
be
misused.

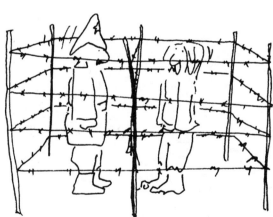

Although my fantasy runs away with me, the concept of the boundary emerges clearly. I am satisfied.

The boundary of the self could be called the obviousness of the senses. The self-boundary goes as far as the eye reaches and touches the surface of objects. The senses touch. They don't penetrate the surface. To go deeper we have to destroy the surface, the obvious. To be in touch means to be surface-oriented. This is one of the major characteristics of Gestalt Therapy.

Without respect for the surface, we penetrate and analyze ad infinitum, for as deeply as we penetrate there will always be encountered another surface. Like an onion, as one layer is peeled off another emerges, and another and another until we reach nothingness.

Freud speaks of repressions and return of the unconscious. If we understand the language of the obvious we don't need this double-talk. Nothing is ever really repressed. All relevant gestalten are emerging, they are on the surface, they are obvious like the emperor's nakedness. Your eyes and ears are aware of them, provided your computer analyzing-thinking has not blinded you, provided you stay with the non-verbal self-expressions, movements, posture, voice, etc. Without aiming at the surface, at the self-boundary, you are hopelessly out of touch—and also the counterpart, out of *reach*—walled off by thick layers of verbiage.

The contact boundary, for instance the ego-boundary, is a far more complicated matter until understood in its simplicity. The ego-boundary is like the bed of Procrustes.

Procrustes was a man in ancient Greece who loved to play the fitting and adjustment game. He had only one bed. Thus if his guest was too long, he cut off his feet, if he was too short he stretched and stretched him until he was adjusted to the length of the bed.

This is what we do to ourselves, if our potential does not fit our self-image.

Not all boundaries are as rigid as that bed. A story from ancient Palestine shows both a rigid and a shifting boundary.

There lived a prostitute in a village. One day the villagers decided to stone her. I don't know the reason. Maybe she had overcharged a customer or had given him VD. In any case, while they were about to stone that girl, a guy came along with a blond beard and long hair, looking like a clean hippy. He lifted his right forefinger and pronounced: "He who is without sin shall throw the first stone." Everybody dropped his stone. Silence. Then "bang" came a single stone.

The girl turned around: "M O T H E R!"

What happened? There is no interruption in the mother's behavior. But the rest? Did they suddenly get inhibited? Did they calculate the equation sin = sin? Did they realize their projection? All this is possible, but misses the point. The point is that they woke up from a trance of fury, that they got in touch with reality, that they had some sort of a *satori* experience.

We have glorious Indian Summer weather. A bit too hot. I had a short siesta, woke up from a vivid dream saying goodbye to the Rund family, my mother's family. Saying goodbye to my grandfather seems irrevocable. I will see the others again but not him. I am sitting quite a distance from him, kiss his hand and realize he is sitting there and I have an arm next to me with no person attached. A very manly arm.

I am bored and yawning. I am too lazy to do something with this arm.

Boredom and tiredness. You helped me before. I don't want to play the dream in the Perls style, nor associate in the Freud style. I want to stay with the atmosphere. The saying goodbye and my reverence for him has something phony, forced.

I am scanning for images, I am yawning, comparing him with my father, comparing my embracing when I am phony and when real. The change in my sexual curiosity is coming up.

My compulsion to look at female genitals, to touch them, to manipulate them, has suddenly changed its character.

I am waking up. Something clicks. The empty compulsive greed = a trance dictated by a power drive—never, never satisfied. Overcompensating a disgust, yet a never-ending curiosity. Peeping with squeamishness and fear of being caught. In the last days I woke up. The peeping has changed into free and guilt-free looking, interested in the different characters of the different cunts.

They tell me much about the personality of each girl, similarly to the much more superficial kiss encounter. The cunt experience is intensive and non-verbal. I am too shy to speak about it. Freedom, nothing sneaky, interested open eyes, no trance, no need to interfere and "make" the girl.

I play grandpa now. I am stern and grumpy. I don't show much love. I am giving Fritz a birthday present. Not just those cheap stamped soldiers on horse. They can mount and dismount. You see the horses have holes and the soldiers something between their legs. You get my message?

Look at the real horses. What a powerful prick. "Look at your own piddling little thing!"

I feel like defending my prick. There was a time it was very big and very powerful, but the time has come to say goodbye.

Grandpa, your death hardly touched me. What about my being a grandfather? I got a letter from Ren with pictures of Leslie for the commencement book. For once a letter without asking me for something, but I am sure the letter is an overture for a request that likely will come via Lore.

The fact is that I like Leslie very much, a cute and bright copperhead. There is something real about her in contrast to her mother's and sister's insincerity.

Teddy and I are always reading over this manuscript before she takes it home for typing. She said she did not understand the difference between the self-boundary and the ego-boundary. I know that I left many loose threads hanging, but I also know that I am not ready to write a systematic account of Gestalt philosophy. I am still discovering, but I also have many parts ready for the total picture. With my first book I violated McLuhan's verdict: "No book will be accepted that contains more than 10% new ideas." This time I don't just want to show off what I know. I want to let you see me, including my search. Perhaps you trust me and I trust myself that eventually both the philosophy and I will become a whole. I am reluctant to say they will be integrated. This term looks like a finality.

Again I have to pull Freud in for comparison. He said at the end of his life, "No analysis can ever be finished," and I say before the end of my life, "There is no end to integration."

He would say: you can always analyze and discover new material.

I say: there is always something you can assimilate and integrate. There is always a chance for growing.

Freud: Integration takes care of itself. If you free the repressions, they become available.

Fritz: They may become available, provided they are not just filed away as interesting insights—I have seen often enough that repressed and liberated material was not worked through as you correctly demanded, but was still alienated and projected. I have seen this most frequently with Reich and the other armor-busters.

Freud: I am not responsible for them.

Fritz: In a way you are. You promoted the "discharge of emotion" theory. You were inconsistent, when in your magnificent work on grief you showed that grief, the mourning labor, is an eminently purposeful survival-promoting process, and not just a discharge.

Teddy: All this talking does not help me. I want to understand the difference between the self-boundary and the ego-boundary.

Fritz: O.K. Now, Teddy, how far do you extend yourself?

T: (pushing her arms up) That far!

F: Now even to the ceiling.

T: I can see the ceiling.

F: Can you see through the ceiling?

T: Of course not.

F: So you reach as far as you can with your arms, with your eyes, and with your ears. Right?

T: Right.

F: No ego involved?

T: Not as far as I can make out.

F: You reach out to the ceiling; you yourself are trying to touch the ceiling?

T: Yes.

F: Is your ego trying to touch the ceiling?

T: That sounds like nonsense. *Obviously* "I" do it.

F: Now you have the self-boundary. The philosophy of the obvious.

I have been cheating in this story and I doubt if any one noticed it. When Teddy tried to reach the ceiling she put on a performance. There was nothing on the ceiling she wanted to reach for. Thus the reaching was an artifact, a demonstration. *Phenomenology is not an easy science.* The emperor seems always to quickly put on some clothes and produce a surface other than his skin.

Although the laws of the ego-boundary apply to all types of social or multi-individual groups, I want, for simplicity's sake, to stick to the individual ego-boundary. Without understanding those laws, all therapy and interpersonal relations remain a gimmick-supported manipulation.

The ego-boundary is the zero point between good and bad, identification and alienation, familiar and strange, right and wrong, self-expression and projection.

We can even cluster the right and the left side terms and put them inside and outside the boundary.

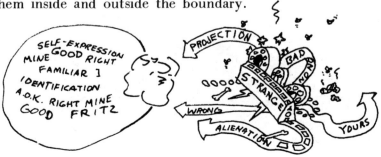

I am coming back again and again to the word "identification." I really have a thing with it. I identify the sensoric system *with* the system of orientation, and orientation is built upon the ability to identify something as X. Without this there is nothing but chaos and confusion. Perception and cognition seem to melt together as the identification process.

A sentry asks a man for the password. "Identify yourself as being identified with us." Identification cards. Fingerprints. Witnesses as means of identifying a criminal. Here the identification serves the polarity of right and wrong. Is he the right man? Only one person can be the right one, a billion the wrong ones.

Identification is familiarity, anti-confusion.

Strangeness is uncanny—no means of orientation. In a small village the foreigner is out of the boundary, an enemy. One does not know his ways. He might have something up his sleeve one cannot cope with.

The psychoanalyst identifies an elongated thing as a penis. This fits his orientation, a system he is familiar with.

A cat identifies a thing as a piece of fish, as belonging to his world of sustenance.

I feel a little bit like Heidegger, getting deep into language to the point where language meets existence. "Identifying" reaches the two systems, the orientation (sensoric) system and the coping (motoric) system. Through the password the sentry identifies his man "as" friend or enemy. He identifies "with" the friend and admits him through the boundary, the *cordon sanitaire*. He rejects or destroys the enemy. The friend is good, the enemy is bad.

The boundary principle reaches from the borders of nations to the behavior of electrons. A condenser has an isolating plate where the positive and negative charges oppose each other.

The contact boundary is also a separation boundary. Inside the boundary things and people take on a positive connotation, outside a negative one. I use "positive" and "negative" in a judgemental sense, "positive" meaning accepting, saying "yes;" negative meaning rejecting, saying "no."

One's own God is the God of the righteous, pious people. Other Gods are the rulers of heathens. The own country's soldiers are heroes and defenders, the opposing army has the attackers and rapists.

"I know all that stuff. Every B-grade movie is full of the good guys and the bad guys. What do we need all the boundary stuff for? And especially: self-boundary versus ego-boundary. That may be a thing for philosophers and semantic people, but not for me. Why don't you give us something more personal, something exciting about your sex life, for instance."

There is not much to talk about there. The only two points worth mentioning are that grandpa stuck with me a while longer, until I realized that he represents working and lack of enjoyment. He lived exclusively inside the boundary of his family and his temple. My father lived mostly outside the family boundary. At home he was a guest, to be served and respected.

My father and mother had many bitter fights, including physical fights, when he beat her and she grabbed his magnificent beard. He often called her a piece of furniture or a piece of shit.

Step by step he isolated himself, as we moved from one place to another.

In Germany all apartment houses had front and court apartments. The front apartments with the view on the street had marble staircases and carpets and an extra entrance for servants. The court apartment in the *Ansbacher Strasse* had at least a little garden and a rod where the servants beat the dust out of the carpets. There was no electricity, thus no vacuum cleaners or refrigerators.

My mother used those carpet beaters on me. She did not break my spirit; I broke the beaters.

I've witnessed the coming about of modern age. The landlord installed electric bells in our house. The juice came from accumulators. They were serviced by my cousin Martin, of whom I was very fond. He was interested in all kinds of handicraft and gadgets, all of which had a great fascination for me. He never seemed to be interested in girls. He committed suicide and I always had the fantasy he did so in despair because he could not lick the "sin" of masturbation.

The trolley cars were horsedrawn, until electricity was installed. When they built the Berlin subway I watched for hours the gigantic hammers driving strong piles into the ground. I watched the first hopping flights of the Wright brothers on the Tempehof Field, which was the Emperor's big parade ground and is now a famous aerodrome. Then the plane races, where they got speeds up to forty miles an hour.

In the meantime, my parents became increasingly alienated while they were creeping up the middle-class ladder. The first apartment was still a rear apartment with four rooms.

Below us lived the widow Freiberg with a son who at first put in a claim to acting, and later to singing. Through him, I got my initiation to the stage. Not quite.

When I was four, I fell in love with a circus horseback rider who seemed to belong to another, wonderful world. Her golden costume, her elegance and self-possession—the princess of the fairytale incarnate. My first goddess to be put on a pedestal.

Was such a world beyond my reach? Maybe not. Soon afterwards, I saw some boys in a sandpit playing circus. I recognized the clown. One day, who knows, one day. . .

Our large living room had a big alcove. The Freiberg boy, Theo, used that to produce a play. Two of my mother's sisters—Aunt Salka and Aunt Clara—were in it. I did not understand a word, but I was allowed to pull the curtain and to do little chores and to watch the rehearsals. He especially loved to rehearse embraces. Though what he got out of squeezing those corset-imprisoned ladies, I could not imagine.

Later, the Punch and Judy shows, the real theater performances, were enjoyed and taken seriously. What kind of people were those actors, who could turn themselves into something different?

When Theo, with the help of my Hebrew teacher, put on an opera performance—*Il Trovatore*—I was disappointed. The stage and props were shabby, they wriggled on the floor and sang to each other. I got my own back by finding it funny. I covered my disappointment by ridiculing his efforts.

We kept in touch, and much later I went with Theo's troupe to small cities to give theater performances of some kind.

I had already invaded the real theater. This was after I had again come to terms with life at the *Askanische Gymnasium*.

They sometimes needed a lot of "extras" for the Royal Theater. An actor was in charge of that. He was allotted half a mark, 12.5 cents, for each, and as we students refused that money, we were very welcome. We loved the costumes and participation and getting acquainted with literature in a lively way.

Sometimes the emperor attended a performance of *Kolberg*, the story of a siege. Then the order would come down: "Twice the usual shouting and hurrahs."

Then I switched my loyalty to the *Deutsche Theater*, where Max Reinhardt was in charge. Max Reinhardt was the first creative genius I met. The writers' dreams had to become real. The painted props had to go. The pompous voices of the hams had to go. Characters out of touch with their co-players had to go. Nothing was left untouched, until a play transcended into a world of reality, yet left enough room for the audience's fantasy.

With infinite patience, he could rehearse co-players until their voices matched and met. He understood the rhythm of tensions and silence, so that prose turned into music. The tragedy of *Oedipus*, played in a large circus with hundreds of people screaming in gong-supported rhythm for help, relentlessly revealing man's guiltless guilt; *A Midsummer Night's Dream* becoming the fairy-est of all tales; the second part of Goethe's *Faust* with its richness of ancient and medieval mythology stretching into six-and-a-half hours of vivid witnessing of history, philosophy, and man's yearning for redemption; the pictorial richness of *Everyman's* encounters with death—all these became life in its utmost intensity, not "just plays."

I had entered a life of multiple existence. One summer, for instance, many days went like this: In the morning, I did my homework in the elevated train on my way to school. From school home for a quick lunch and on my bicycle to an open-air theater, where I had my first contract as an actor. I got five marks per performance, an unheard-of sum for me.

Pocket money was unknown. Before that time, I either had to steal some money from my mother's purse or give tutoring lessons to dunces. Now I could pay for acting lessons and buy myself a motorbike in addition.

After the afternoon performance, cycling back those four miles, sometimes not even going home for supper so as to be on time for the Reinhardt performances, which often lasted deep into the night. My mother trembled lest my father get home before me and make another stink. But this was rare. Either he was somewhere in Germany selling his wine and ideals, or he was out enjoying wine, women and song.

At that time, I was not a good actor and the acting lessons did not do much for me. I was, however, very good at imitating the voices of many famous actors. In other words, I was a good imitator but not at all creative. It was not until five years ago that I discovered my secret for good acting.

That was at a party in Ein Hod in Israel. A number of people performed. I was envious, and when I am envious or jealous, the devil in me takes over. I decided to give them the fright of their lives and to play dying. The trick was to believe that I really was dying. This trick, I believe now, is the basis of hysteria. The thing went off beautifully. Gosh, were they worried and concerned—until I took a bow, and got them very angry. Now I am a good actor and performer, easily achieving a chameleon-like transformation. I bring much joy to many people, mostly with my clowning.

I am bored and disgruntled again. After I worked somewhat on the grandpa dream, I saw that I have every reason to be satisfied. I have some fame, money, friends, talents. The work on my own pathology progresses well. The deadly boredom disappeared after I invested in this writing. It is now back in a diminished form. Now and then, when I enjoy my cruelty—as in warfare with an army of ants marching relentlessly and indestructibly as a tribe, undermining my house or at least eating my goodies—I feel alive and involved.

When I concentrate on my schizophrenic layer, I can more and more stay alert and witness the thousand phenomena coming up. But then I either fall asleep or get so restless and excited that I often cannot tolerate that excitement and wander about lost in confusion without the anchorage of involvement.

For a while, I thought this time I would lick my typing block and got up to a speed of about 50/60 words per minute—then I messed it up and lost interest again.

I am becoming very aware of the devil in me, passing poisonous righteous judgements. I am still stuck. I am listening to the Brahms clarinet quintet. No, I am not listening, I am just hearing it; I am not involved. Now, of course, it begins to occupy my interest and the writing is getting depersonalized and heavy. Okay, Brahms; I surrender. I lost my boredom.

I am most interested in the two phenomena of projection and pain. If we stick to the oversimplification of topology, of placing and moving about in space, we observe again and again that every one of us tries to keep the region within the boundary as harmonious and pleasant as possible. In order to do this we have to cleanse the ego.

I want to go back to the beginning of the book, to the differentiation between the authenticity of self-actualization and the distortion of self-image; between what we are as our inherited potential and the desire to become what we are supposed to be; between being and manufactured achievement; between spontaneity and deliberatness.

I wrote those two paragraphs about ten days ago. Then I lost my urge to write. I gave a workshop for the "blowout center" staff and a weekend seminar. I also had some good ideas which I wrote down only in fantasy. The rationalization was, of course, "What's the use," forgetting conveniently that I am writing for my needs and not for mankind.

I told Dick Price that I am working towards a life of non-commitment. That I am interested—nay fascinated—to solve the riddle of schizophrenia. I believe one case, fully understood, will do more than the research and examination of hundreds of cases and control cases. In this respect I follow Kurt Goldstein and Sigmund Freud completely. What I miss in both is the appreciation of role-playing. Goldstein's research is essentially centered around coping. How does Schneider, his famous case, perform when given a task? What makes him *perform* in the first case? I am switching back to the performance of the encephalitis case when he was asked to drink a glass of water without being thirsty. When he does this as a *performance*, that is, as a deliberate act of phony behavior, he does so with shaking and strain. When he is authentic, spontaneous, not performing, he drinks his water with ease and comfort. If the theory is correct, that a brain-injured person has no categorical way of thinking, then the answer has to be, "I don't want to, I have no need to comply."

One thing seems to be sure. Like with all obscure phenomena, we have a given answer. The only difficulty is to ask the
right question.

Ken Price is leaving today to take over the care of our first
kibbutz property. On the surface it looks like an inconsistency if
I say that I do not want to commit myself to any further
projects and talk at the same time about investigating schizophrenia and starting the first Gestalt kibbutz.

When I commit myself I am very reliable. I can make an
appointment at any place in the States at any specific time and
I'll be there. I still have a number of workshops and seminars to
do; I promised a month's presence at the Santa Barbara U.C.
campus. I have one more circuit of workshops and lectures from
Florida to Vancouver lasting six weeks, and then I will be free
from commitments and I leave the future open, dependent upon
the political development and my interest.

In the meantime, I am full of fantasies and plans, full of
possibilities and lack of certainties. Anything can happen, including death.

I escaped death often in my life and many times I craved
for it. At present, I find life so full of promises and risks that I
am rather fond of it.

One of the silliest ways I nearly killed myself happened
during my first solo flight. Nowadays you fly your tricycle
under-carriage right to the ground. We had to land by correct
stalling of the plane. I was unsure that time, made a bad landing
and decided to go on immediately. But then the bloody crate
did not want to leave the ground and there was the forest on
the edge of the aerodome looming ahead of me. Finally I leave
the ground, sure to crash into the tree-tops and just manage to
clear them. I looked back. My instructor is there waving his arms
wildly. I turn around and make a good landing. He points to the
propeller. I don't trust my eyes. There is hardly any propeller
left. With the pump-handling of the first landing I had smashed
it, and (what a plane!) managed at an altitude of six thousand
feet (Johannesburg) to get that thing airborne with that stump
that had been a propeller.

Living at that altitude never bothered me nor did flying up another few thousand feet in an open cockpit. At that time I had no apparent trouble with my heart. But now?

The proposed kibbutz is 7500 feet high in New Mexico. This might be a strain.

What do I mean by Gestalt kibbutz? As I had previously considered individual therapy to be obsolete, so I now consider the piecemeal group meeting and workshops to be out-of-date. The marathon meetings are too forced.

I propose now to conduct the following experiment. In the kibbutz, the split between seminarians and staff has to be abolished. All the work has to be done by the people coming to the kibbutz. Permanent staff: 1) the caretaker and developer, someone who has a background of ranching and building, etc. 2) the therapist.

The main accent is on developing a community spirit and maturation. People are meant to go there for three months, initially for a fee of $1000 for that period. There will be a turnover every month of ten leaving and ten arriving. There will be organic and vegetable farming and a craft shop for making simple furniture.

We have a good house there, but additional buildings will be required. Once this is done the fee can be lowered, perhaps eventually altogether abolished.

This first kibbutz is meant to be a leader-breeder place. I have already several professional therapists signed up.

If this experiment works, there should be coming places for families, non-professional singles, teenagers, black and white, Birchers and hippies.

Who knows? It might eventually spread into the ghettos and other places where constructive living would be welcomed.

Tonight I finally feel some impulse to write. Some more pieces are falling into place. The differentiation of our relation to the world into the sensoric and motoric system is making more and more sense. I was preoccupied the last week with listening, mainly to music, and the motoric urge to write, to do, to talk, got less bio-energy. I have now had several cases of compulsive motoric behavior up to the point of obsession and paranoia (they are very closely related), and in all those cases there was a lack of feeling.

This will be useful for the understanding of the extreme poles in schizophrenia: the paranoiac motoric lacking sensitivity, and the withdrawn sensitive with his lack of purposeful motoric activity. I also know that I am right not to suppress my smoking habit. Whenever I am avoiding some unpleasant feeling the energy goes into moving, and the cigarette, of course, is the handiest excuse.

As the enthusiasm for writing declines, my topdog takes over and nags me to finish this book, to pull the loose ends together and find a way to make my ideas more easily understandable. I am thinking, for instance, of the Indian word *maya*—in European philosophy, the philosophy of "as if." *Maya* is to be contrasted with *reality*, the observable common world. The two can be miles apart, which is insanity, or they can be integrated, which is art. All fantasy, thinking, game-and role-playing, dreams, novels, etc. would be part of it. Most important is the illusion of the ego and its boundary.

The account of the function of the boundary is nearly complete, but we have to add two more phenomena: esthetics and ownership.

The poles of esthetic behavior are similarly fated as the moral issues; everything beautiful belongs inside the boundary, and everything ugly, outside. The German word for ugly is *haesslich*, hateful. Love and beauty are nearly identical.

Richard III is like many "abnormal" cases, a reversal of the normal boundary. "As I am ugly, I might just as well be a villain and hate beauty and goodness."

Perhaps easiest to understand is the feeling of ownership within the boundary. Everything within the boundary is "mine," belonging, properly esteemed. Everything outside is yours, not mine, be it things or attitudes. Envy or greed might want to include something outside into one's boundary and one wants to get rid of things and attitudes inside which are experienced as ugly, toxic, bad, weak, crazy, stupid, strange, symptoms, and yet, in the case of sanity, to be identified as mine.

This is the metabolism that leads to introjections: falsification of self by appearing to be more than one is. In repressions and projections there is also falsification of self: appearing to be less than one is. This metabolism is meant to avoid pain, discomfort, pseudo-suffering.

Now we finally see emerge the picture of health, neurosis and psychosis. The extreme cases are rare and about everyone participates somewhat in all three possibilities.

In health we are in touch with the world and with our own self, that is, with reality.

In a psychosis we are out of touch with reality, and in touch with *maya*, a delusion system essentially centered around the ego, for instance the frequent symptoms of megalomania and worthlessness.

In a neurosis a continual fight between ego and self, between delusion and reality, is taking place.

The delusional system works like a cancer, absorbing more and more of the vital energy and progressively saps the strength of the living organism. The severity of the mental illness depends on the identification function with either ego or self. The psychotic says, "I am Abraham Lincoln," the neurotic person: "I would like to be like Abraham Lincoln," the healthy one: "I am what I am."

The treatment procedure now becomes obvious. We have to drain the delusional system, the middle zone, the ego, the complexes, and put that energy at the disposal of the self, so that the organism can grow and use his innate potential.

During this procedure we can observe how the holes in the personality disappear and how that person becomes a well-functioning whole again.

Sigmund Freud: "Dr. Perls, you are not telling me anything new. Only your formulation is different. I can explain my approach in your language too. If a person is sexually impotent, you would say that instead of genitals he has a void. The excitement goes, instead of into his genitals, into the oral and anal zone where it creates a lot of disturbances like perversions and character features. Once the libido flows into the genital zone, the other zones are free for their organismic functions, undisturbed by the intruding libido. The genitals become alive, and function correctly biologically—and possibly even sociologically. Maturation and health have been accomplished. The void is filled."

Fritz: I am glad that we found a common operational basis. I sure admire the tenacity you displayed to salvage sex from its sinful status in Western culture. You set the pattern to fill other holes, too: the many discoveries you made during your lifetime, discoveries that became indispensable tools for our research.

We have, indeed, to reformulate your 19th century approach with its limited intellectual tools, to fit the 20th century. You would easily agree with me that there are many holes to fill.

Actually you saw at least another hole clearly: amnesia. You used the image, borrowed from reality, of the censor who forbids certain paragraphs to appear in the newspapers and pointed to the white nothingness that appeared instead of the print.

I borrowed that example from you to illustrate the neurotic man of our time: the incomplete, insipid personality with holes instead of relevant messages that count.

The emphasis is now shifting from attending to specific symptoms, character features, and conflicts, to a witch-hunt for the void, hole, empty space, nothingness, incompleteness.

Your specific *means whereby* for the void production is repression. We have to enlarge that to *any* kind of avoidance: withdrawing of attention, phobic attitudes, fixation on irrelevant issues, distortion of the gestalt formation, desensitivity, mental fog, etc.

Thus the question: "What are you avoiding?" is very much in vogue in Gestalt Therapy and becomes the basic attitude in our dreamwork.

The fundamental issue for us existentialists is, of course, the whole of self, authenticity, of being real and all there.

This whole of self is replaced and substituted by the *maya* of the ego. As Alan Watts said the other day of somebody: "He is nothing but an ego with a skin wrapped around it."

To make this fundamental issue perfectly clear, let's take once more an extreme example, such as the encephalitis case. There we contrasted the deliberate *ego*-function shakingly reaching for the glass of water, with the ease of *self*-functioning if dictated by the gestalt formation of thirst.

In alcoholism we see sometimes the Korsakoff syndrome of amnesia. The patient is not aware of his memory hole and replaces it with fantasies. He fills the sterile void with falsified memories.

Thus the more of the authentic self is missing, the more we fill that hole with functions. The less contact and support the ego receives from the self, the greater the phoniness and paper-mache character of the ego.

During my analysis with Clara Happel, I had one of the few

real experiences I ever got from psychoanalysis. Lots of my directional support came from my topdog. When this collapsed, I walked the streets of Frankfurt for several nights, lost, not knowing what to do. There was a hole instead of an autonomous direction or acceptable outer direction. I did not trust her, nor did I trust myself.

Will I ever learn to trust myself completely?

Gestalt Institute of Canada
Lake Cowichan, B.C.

July 1969

I wrote The Garbage Pail in three months and after that—nothing. Just as suddenly as the urge to write appeared, I dried up.

I have embarked on a new adventure—a therapeutic community. The kibbutz has not materialized as yet. I have made beautiful films with Aquarian Productions in Vancouver, and occasionally I imagine that I will write again.

Right now, reality demands all my excitement and little is left for verbiage. You can find plenty of verbiage in *Gestalt Therapy Verbatim,* and if you want to listen to me, you can hear me on the tapes from which John Stevens created that book.

Fritz Perls.